... ine Zufriedenheit zu bitten; —
... Lüntzigau Monath 100 fl: Lohnen, und
... nur das Quartal meines gage
... dindas Günstigsetzten worden. —
... erbrent zu schelten hab, und gab
... Minuten noch nicht schelten; Sie ...
... dom gelte entblößt, so daß ...
... und das wegen mein Hochman
... Schcht gäntzlich überzängt bei, ;
... gehörnen Kommen ...
...
... —

Mozart

MOZART
LETTERS

Translated by Lady Wallace
Selected and edited by Peter Washington
and Michael Rose

EVERYMAN'S LIBRARY

Alfred A. Knopf New York London Toronto

THIS IS A BORZOI BOOK
PUBLISHED BY ALFRED A. KNOPF

This selection by Peter Washington and Michael Rose first published in
Everyman's Library, 2006 (UK), 2007 (US)
Copyright © 2006, 2007 by Everyman's Library

www.randomhouse.com/everymans
www.everymanslibrary.co.uk

ISBN 978-0-307-26625-5 (US)
978-1-84159-773-7 (UK)

A CIP catalogue record for this book is available from the British Library

Typography by Peter B. Willberg
Typeset in the UK by AccComputing, North Barrow, Somerset
Printed and bound in Germany by GGP Media GmbH, Pössneck

FOREWORD

How Mozart found the time to be such a prolific and brilliant letter writer will always remain as much of a mystery as his musical genius. After more than two hundred years he still stands out as one of music's greatest correspondents, emerging from the pages which follow as a scintillating, fully rounded and intriguing character. About 1200 of the letters which passed between Mozart, his family and friends have survived, the most important of them written by the composer and his father. This selection is based on the translation by Lady Wallace first published in 1865, with extra material supplied by the editors. Despite their date, Lady Wallace's versions of the text are frank, lively and usually faithful. However, she did not have access to some of Mozart's later letters to Constanze. From tact or ignorance, she also omitted all but the mildest of his scatalogical references. A few of these have been restored by the editors to give a fuller picture of the man. We have also included relevant letters by Leopold Mozart not translated by Lady Wallace. Leopold exerted profound influence, not to say control, over Wolfgang until the old man died, only four years before his celebrated son. This epistolary portrait is completed by Barrington's description of the composer as a child prodigy, and an account of Mozart's last hours by his wife's youngest sister, Sophie.

THE LETTERS
1762–91

Mozart's father, Leopold, aware that his son was something out of the ordinary as a musical prodigy, was eager to exhibit his amazing abilities to as wide a public as possible. For this purpose it was necessary to get away from the provincial world of Salzburg (where Leopold held an appointment in the Archbishop's Court), and throughout his childhood Wolfgang Mozart was constantly travelling, sometimes with his father and sister, later just with his mother, from one great European city to another. The first journey, to Munich in January 1762, was undertaken without Frau Mozart and has left no documentary record, but the second, to Vienna later in the same year, included the whole family. At this time Mozart was six and a half years old, his sister Nannerl just turned eleven.

Leopold Mozart to Lorenz Hagenauer, Salzburg
Vienna, 16 October 1762

... On the feast of St. Francis we left Linz at half past four in the afternoon by the so-called ordinary boat and reached Mauthausen after nightfall on the same day at half past seven. At noon on the following day, Tuesday, we arrived at Ybbs, where two Minorites and a Benedictine, who were with us on the boat, said Masses, during which our Woferl played so well on the organ that the Franciscans, who happened to be entertaining

9

some guests at their midday meal, left the table and with their company rushed to the choir and were almost struck dead with astonishment. In the evening we reached Stein and on Wednesday at three in the afternoon arrived at Vienna; here at five o'clock we took our midday meal and supper at the same time. On the journey we had continual rain and wind. Wolfgang had already caught a cold in Linz, but in spite of our irregular life, early rising, eating and drinking at all hours, and wind and rain, he has, thank God, kept well. When we landed, Gilowsky's servant, who was already there, came on board and brought us to our lodgings. But after leaving our luggage safely and tidily there, we soon hurried off to an inn to sate our hunger. Gilowsky himself then came to welcome us. Now we have already been here five days and do not yet know where the sun rises in Vienna, for to this very hour it has done nothing but rain and, with constant wind, has snowed a little now and then, so that we have even seen some snow on the roofs. Moreover it has been and remains very frosty, though not excessively cold. One thing I must make a point of telling you, which is, that we quickly got through the local customs and were let off the chief customs altogether. And for this we have to thank our Master Woferl. For he made friends at once with the customs officer, showed him his clavier, invited him to visit us and played him a minuet on his little fiddle. Thus we got through. The customs officer asked most politely to be allowed to visit us and for this purpose made a note of our lodgings. So far, in spite of the most atrocious weather, we have been to a concert given by Count Collalto. Further, Countess Sinzendorf introduced us to Count Wilschegg and on the 11th to His Excellency the Imperial Vice-Chancellor, Count Colloredo, where we were privileged to see and to speak to the leading ministers and ladies of the Imperial Court, to wit, the Hungarian Chancellor, Count Palffy, and the Bohemian Chancellor, Count Chotek, as well as Bishop Esterházy and a number of persons, all of whom I cannot record. All, especially the ladies, were very gracious to us. Count Leopold Kühnburg's fiancée spoke to my wife of her own accord and told her that she is going to be married at Salzburg. She is a pretty, friendly woman, of medium height. She is expecting her betrothed in Vienna very shortly. Countess Sinzendorf is using her influence on our behalf, and all the ladies are in love with my boy. We are already being talked of everywhere: and when on the 10th I was alone at the opera, I heard the Archduke Leopold from his box say a number of things to another box, namely, that there was a boy in Vienna who played the clavier most excellently and so on. At eleven o'clock that very same evening I received a command to go to Schönbrunn on the 12th. But the following day there came a fresh command to go there on the 13th instead (the 12th being the Feast of Maximilian and therefore a very busy gala-day), because,

I understand, they want to hear the children in comfort. Everyone is amazed, especially at the boy, and everyone whom I have heard says that his genius is unbelievable. Baron Schell is using his influence on my behalf and is gratefully acknowledging the kindnesses he enjoyed at Salzburg. If you have a chance, please tell this to Herr Chiusolis with my respects. Count Daun also has given me a note for Baron Schell and has filled me with hopes that I shall leave Vienna fully content. And so it seems, since the Court is asking to hear us before we have announced ourselves. For young Count Palffy happened to be passing through Linz as our concert was about to begin. He was calling on the Countess Schlick, who told him about the boy and persuaded him to stop the mail coach in front of the town hall and attend the concert with her. He listened with astonishment and spoke later with great excitement of the performance to the Archduke Joseph, who told the Empress. Thus, as soon as it was known that we were in Vienna, the command came for us to go to court. That, you see, is how it happened.

I wrote the above on the 11th, fully intending to tell you on the 12th, after our return from Schönbrunn, how everything had proceeded. But we had to drive from Schönbrunn straight to Prince von Hildburghausen, and six ducats were more important to us than the despatch of my letter. I have sufficient confidence in Frau Hagenauer and trust enough to her kind friendship to know that she will accept even now our congratulations on her name-day and even in the short form of merely saying that we shall ask God to keep her and all her loved ones well and strong for many years to come and to invite us all in due course to play cards in Heaven. Now all that I have time for is to say hastily that Their Majesties received us with such extraordinary graciousness that, if I describe it, people will declare that I have made it up. Suffice it to say that Woferl jumped up on the Empress's lap, put his arms round her neck and kissed her heartily. In short, we were there from three to six o'clock and the Emperor himself came out of the next room and made me go in there to hear the Infanta play the violin. On the 15th the Empress sent us by the Privy Paymaster, who drove up to our house in state, two dresses, one for the boy and one for the girl. As soon as the command arrives, they are to appear at court and the Privy Paymaster will fetch them. Today at half past two in the afternoon they are to go to the two youngest Archdukes and at four o'clock to the Hungarian Chancellor, Count Palffy. Yesterday we were with Count Kaunitz, and the day before with Countess Kinsky and later with the Count von Ulefeld. And we already have more engagements for the next two days. Please tell everybody that, thank God, we are well and happy. I send greetings and I am your old

Mozart

The Mozarts returned to Salzburg early in January 1763, but in June the whole family were off again – this time on a full European tour, first visiting a number of cities in southern Germany, spending the winter of 1763–4 in Paris, and fetching up in London for the rest of 1764 and a good part of the next year. The following report, received by the Secretary of the Royal Society in London in 1769, describes Mozart towards the end of this London visit, at the age of nine (though his father, ever with an eye to the main chance, continued to trim his age by a year for the purpose of public appearances in the city).

Account of a Very Remarkable Young Musician

*In a Letter from the Honourable Daines Barrington, F.R.S.
to Mathew Maty, M.D. Sec. R.S. Read Feb. 15, 1770*

Sir,

If I was to send you a well attested account of a boy who measured seven feet in height, when he was not more than eight years of age, it might be considered as not undeserving the notice of the Royal Society.

The instance which I now desire you will communicate to that learned body, of as early an exertion of most extraordinary musical talents, seems perhaps equally to claim their attention.

Joannes Chrysostomus Wolfgangus Theophilus Mozart, was born at Saltzbourg in Bavaria, on the 17th of January, 1756. [See footnote opposite.]

14

I have been informed by a most able musician and composer, that he frequently saw him at Vienna, when he was little more than four years old.

By this time he not only was capable of executing lessons on his favourite instrument the harpsichord, but composed some in an easy stile and taste, which were much approved of.

His extraordinary musical talents soon reached the ears of the present empress dowager, who used to place him upon her knees whilst he played on the harpsichord.

This notice taken of him by so great a personage, together with a certain conciousness of his most singular abilities, had much emboldened the little musician. Being therefore the next year at one of the German courts, where the elector encouraged him, by saying,

---

I here subjoin a copy of the translation from the register at Saltzbourg, as it was procured from his excellence Count Haslang, envoy extraordinary and minister plenipotentiary of the electors of Bavaria and Palatine:

'I, the under-written, certify, that in the year 1756, the 17th of January, at eight o'clock in the evening, was born Joannes Chrysostomus Wolfgangus Theophilus, son of Mr. Leopold Mozart, organist of his highness the prince of Saltzbourg, and of Maria Ann his lawful wife (whose maiden name was Pertlin), and christened the day following, at ten o'clock in the morning, at the prince's cathedral church here; his godfather being Gottlieb Pergmayr, merchant in this city. In truth whereof, I have taken this certificate from the parochial register of christenings, and under the usual seal, signed the same with my own hand.

Saltzbourg,   Leopald Comprecht,
Jan. 3, 1769.   Chaplain to his Highness in this city.'

15

that he had nothing to fear from his august presence; Little Mozart immediately sat down with great confidence to his harpsichord, informing his highness, that he had played before the empress.

At seven years of age his father carried him to Paris, where he so distinguished himself by his compositions, that an engraving was made of him.

The father and sister who are introduced in this print, are excessively like their portraits, as is also little Mozart, who is stiled 'Compositeur et Maitre de Musique, agé de sept ans'.

After the name of the engraver, follows the date, which is in 1764; Mozart was therefore at this time in the eighth year of his age.

Upon leaving Paris, he came over to England, where he continued more than a year. As during this time I was witness of his most extraordinary abilities as a musician, both at some publick concerts, and likewise by having been alone with him for a considerable time at his father's house; I send you the following account, amazing and incredible almost as it may appear.

I carried to him a manuscript duet, which was composed by an English gentleman to some favourite words in Metastasio's opera of Demofoonte.

The whole score was in five parts, viz. accompaniments for a first and second violin, the two vocal parts, and a base. I shall here likewise mention, that the parts for the first and second voice were written in what the

Italians stile the *Contralto* cleff; the reason for taking notice of which particular will appear hereafter.

My intention in carrying with me this manuscript composition, was to have an irrefragable proof of his abilities, as a player at sight, it being absolutely impossible that he could have ever seen the music before.

The score was no sooner put upon his desk, than he began to play the symphony in a most masterly manner, as well as in the time and stile which corresponded with the intention of the composer.

I mention this circumstance, because the greatest masters often fail in these particulars on the first trial.

The symphony ended, he took the upper part, leaving the under one to his father.

His voice in the tone of it was thin and infantine, but nothing could exceed the masterly manner in which he sung.

His father, who took the under part in this duet, was once or twice out, though the passages were not more difficult than those in the upper one; on which occasions the son looked back with some anger pointing out to him his mistakes, and setting him right.

He not only however did complete justice to the duet, by singing his own part in the truest taste, and with the greatest precision: he also threw in the accompaniments of the two violins, wherever they were most necessary, and produced the best effects.

It is well known that none but the most capital

musicians are capable of accompanying in this superior stile.

As many of those who may be present, when this letter may have the honour of being read before the society, may not possibly be acquainted with the difficulty of playing thus from a musical score, I will endeavour to explain it by the most similar comparison I can think of.

I must at the same time admit, that the illustration will fail in one particular, as the voice in reading cannot comprehend more than what is contained in a single line. I must suppose, however, that the reader's eye, by habit and quickness, may take in other lines, though the voice cannot articulate them, as the musician accompanies the words of an air by his harpsichord.

Let it be imagined, therefore, that a child of eight years old was directed to read five lines* at once, in four** of which the letters of the alphabet were to have different powers.

For example, in the first line A, to have its common powers.

In the second that of B. In the third of C. In the fourth of D.

---

* By this I mean, The two parts for the violins. The upper part for the voice. The words set to music. And lastly, the base.
** By this I mean, The violin parts in the common treble cleff. The upper part for the voice in the contralto cleff as before-mentioned. The words in common characters. And the base in its common cleff.

Let it be conceived also, that the lines so composed of characters, with different powers, are not ranged so as to be read at all times one exactly under the other, but often in a desultory manner.

Suppose then, a capital speech in Shakespeare* never seen before, and yet read by a child of eight years old, with all the pathetic energy of a Garrick.

Let it be conceived likewise, that the same child is reading, with a glance of his eye, three different comments on this speech tending to its illustration; and that one comment is written in Greek, the second in Hebrew, and the third in Etruscan characters.

Let it be also supposed, that by different signs he could point out which comment is most material upon every word; and sometimes that perhaps all three are so, at others only two of them.

When all this is conceived, it will convey some idea of what this boy was capable of, in singing such a duet at sight in a masterly manner from the score, throwing in at the same time all its proper accompaniments.

When he had finished the duet, he expressed himself highly in its approbation, asking with some eagerness whether I had brought any more such music.

Having been informed, however, that he was often visited with musical ideas, to which, even in the midst of the night, he would give utterance on his harpsichord;

* The words in Metastasio's duet, which Mozart sung, are very pathetic.

I told his father that I should be glad to hear some of his extemporary compositions.

The father shook his head at this, saying, that it depended entirely upon his being as it were musically inspired, but that I might ask him whether he was in humour for such a composition.

Happening to know that little Mozart was much taken notice of by Manzoli, the famous singer, who came over to England in 1764, I said to the boy, that I should be glad to hear an extemporary *Love Song*, such as his friend Manzoli might choose in an opera.

The boy on this (who continued to sit at his harpsichord) looked back with much archness, and immediately began five or six lines of a jargon recitative proper to introduce a love song.

He then played a symphony which might correspond with an air composed to the single word, *Affetto*.

It had a first and second part, which, together with the symphonies, was of the length that opera songs generally last: if this extemporary composition was not amazingly capital, yet it was really above mediocrity, and shewed most extraordinary readiness of invention.

Finding that he was in humour, and as it were inspired, I then desired him to compose a *Song of Rage*, such as might be proper for the opera stage.

The boy again looked back with much archness, and began five or six lines of a jargon recitative proper to precede a *Song of Anger*.

This lasted also about the same time with the *Song of Love*; and in the middle of it, he had worked himself up to such a pitch, that he beat his harpsichord like a person possessed, rising sometimes in his chair.

The word he pitched upon for this second extemporary composition was, *Perfido*.

After this he played a difficult lesson, which he had finished a day or two before:* his execution was amazing, considering that his little fingers could scarcely reach a fifth on the harpsichord.

His astonishing readiness, however, did not arise merely from great practice; he had a thorough knowledge of the fundamental principles of composition, as, upon producing a treble, he immediately wrote a base under it, which, when tried, had very good effect.

He was also a great master of modulation, and his transitions from one key to another were excessively natural and judicious; he practised in this manner for a considerable time with an handkerchief over the keys of the harpsichord.

* He published six sonatas for the harpsichord, with an accompaniment for the violin, or German flute, which are sold by R. Bremner, in the Strand, and are intituled, Oeuvre Trois*me*.

He is said in the title page to have been only eight years of age when he composed these sonatas.

The dedication is to the Queen, and is dated at London, January 8, 1765.

He subscribes himself, 'tres humble, et tres obeissant *petit* serviteur'.

These lessons are composed in a very original stile, and some of them are masterly.

The facts which I have been mentioning I was myself an eye witness of; to which I must add, that I have been informed by two or three able musicians, when Bach the celebrated composer had begun a fugue and left off abruptly, that little Mozart hath immediately taken it up, and worked it after a most masterly manner.

Witness as I was myself of most of these extraordinary facts, I must own that I could not help suspecting his father imposed with regard to the real age of the boy, though he had not only a most childish appearance, but likewise had all the actions of that stage of life.

For example, whilst he was playing to me, a favourite cat came in, upon which he immediately left his harpsichord, nor could we bring him back for a considerable time.

He would also sometimes run about the room with a stick between his legs by way of a horse.

I found likewise that most of the London musicians were of the same opinion with regard to his age, not believing it possible that a child of so tender years could surpass most of the masters in that science.

I have therefore for a considerable time made the best inquiries I was able from some of the German musicians resident in London, but could never receive any further information than he was born near Saltzbourg, till I was so fortunate as to procure an extract from the register of that place, through his excellence count Haslang.

It appears from this extract, that Mozart's father did

not impose with regard to his age when he was in England, for it was in June, 1765, that I was witness to what I have above related, when the boy was only eight years and five months old.

I have made frequent inquiries with regard to this very extraordinary genius since he left England, and was told last summer, that he was then at Saltzbourg, where he had composed several oratorios, which were much admired.

I am also informed, that the prince of Saltzbourg, not crediting that such masterly compositions were really those of a child, shut him up for a week, during which he was not permitted to see any one, and was left only with music paper, and the words of an oratorio.

During this short time he composed a very capital oratorio, which was most highly approved of upon being performed ...

His extemporary compositions also, of which I was a witness, prove his genius and invention to have been most astonishing; lest however I should insensibly become too strongly his panegyrist, permit me to subscribe myself, Sir,

Your most faithful
humble servant,
Daines Barrington

The Mozart family arrived home from their European tour at the end of November 1766, a fact noted* by Beda Hübner, the Librarian of St. Peter's Abbey, Salzburg, in his 'Diarium'.

... it is easy to imagine the amount of money this Herr Mozart must have made in England, where moreover all presents are given purely and solely in ready cash. In England too they stayed a whole year, and Herr Mozart in particular, who has in any case a very learned head and possesses great knowledge, as well as a very exalted mind and energetic disposition, acquired a complete knowledge of the English language, having already known Italian and French by reason of his art. From England they went to Holland, and that at the request of the Republic, where again they received very many presents and collected much money. And there again, Herr Mozart, having once learnt the English language, acquired Dutch quite easily. From Holland they went to Switzerland, then to Augsburg, Bavaria, and so on, until at last they once again arrived back at Salzburg in good health, at the keenest desire of the whole town, to the solace, joy and pleasure of everybody of high and low degree, and to their own honour, fame and praise; although nearly all the members of the whole family, especially the wife in England, now and

* A little inaccurately: it was Mozart's father, not his mother, who was ill, and Nannerl was by this time fifteen, not thirteen, years old.

again suffered very dangerous and almost fatal illnesses. The boy is now rather over 10 years of age and the little daughter over 13: the boy Wolfgangl, by the way, has not grown very much during this journey, but Nannerl has become tolerably tall and almost marriageable already. There is a strong rumour that the Mozart family will again not long remain here, but will soon visit the whole of Scandinavia and the whole of Russia, and perhaps even travel to China, which would be a far greater journey and bigger undertaking still.

Russia and China being apparently shelved for the time being, the family's next undertaking was a second visit to Vienna, where they stayed for sixteen months and Mozart, having survived smallpox, was presented at court and saw his little opera Bastien und Bastienne *performed at the private theatre of the famous Dr. Mesmer – though another,* La finta semplice, *did not achieve performance. They were back in Salzburg again for most of 1769, but at the end of that year Mozart and his father set out on another, more ambitious tour, this time with Italy as the objective. They travelled down through Verona to Milan and then on via Bologna to Florence, Rome and Naples, returning over the same ground to Milan where Mozart had been commissioned to write an* opera (Mitridate, rè di Ponto) *for the carnival season of 1770–71. Mozart was nearly fourteen when they set out, and the first of his own letters date from this trip.*

Mozart to his Mother
(a postscript to a letter of his father's)
Wörgl, 14 December 1769

Dearest Mamma!

My heart is completely enchanted with all these pleasures, because it is so jolly on this journey, because it is so warm in the carriage and because our coachman is a fine fellow who, when the road gives him the slightest chance, drives so fast. Papa will have described the journey to Mamma already. The reason why I am writing to Mamma is to show her that I know my duty and that I am with the deepest respect her devoted son

Wolfgang Mozart

Mozart to his Sister (a second postscript)
Wörgl, 14 December 1769

My Dearest Sister,

Thank God, we have arrived safely at Wörgl. To tell the truth, I must say that travelling is very jolly, that it is not at all cold and that it is as warm in our carriage as in a room. How is your sore throat? Surely our Signore Seccatore turned up the very day we left? If you see Herr von Schiedenhofen, tell him that I am always singing 'Tralaliera, Tralaliera' and that I need not put sugar in my soup now that I am no longer in Salzburg. At Lofer we supped and slept in the house of Herr Helmreich, who is prefect there. His wife is an excellent lady. She is the sister of Herr Moll. I am hungry. I am longing to eat something. Meanwhile, farewell. Addio.

PS. – My compliments to all my good friends, to Herr Hagenauer (the merchant), his wife, his sons and his daughters, to Madame Rosa and her husband, to Herr Adlgasser and Herr Spitzeder. As for Herr Hornung, ask him from me whether he has again made the mistake of thinking that I was in bed instead of you.

Wolfgang Mozart

Mozart to his Sister
Milan, 26 January 1770

I rejoice in my heart that you were so well amused at the sledging party you write to me about, and I wish you a thousand opportunities of pleasure, so that you may pass your life merrily. But one thing vexes me, which is, that you allowed Herr von Mölk [an admirer of this pretty young girl of eighteen] to sigh and to sentimentalise, and that you did not go with him in his sledge, that he might have upset you. What a lot of pocket-handkerchiefs he must have used that day to dry the tears he shed for you! He no doubt, too, swallowed at least three ounces of cream of tartar to drive away the horrid evil humours in his body. I know nothing new except that Herr Gellert, the Leipzig poet,* is dead,

* Old Mozart prized Gellert's poems so highly, that on one occasion he wrote to him expressing his admiration.

and has written no more poetry since his death. Just before beginning this letter I composed an air from the 'Demetrio' of Metastasio, which begins thus, 'Misero tu non sei'.

The opera at Mantua was very good. They gave 'Demetrio'. The *prima donna* sings well, but is inanimate, and if you did not see her acting, but only singing, you might suppose she was not singing at all, for she can't open her mouth, and whines out everything; but this is nothing new to us. The *seconda donna* looks like a grenadier, and has a very powerful voice; she really does not sing badly, considering that this is her first appearance. *Il primo uomo, il musico*, sings beautifully, but his voice is uneven; his name is Caselli. *Il secondo uomo* is quite old, and does not at all please me. The tenor's name is Ottini; he does not sing unpleasingly, but with effort, like all Italian tenors. We know him very well. The name of the second I don't know; he is still young, but nothing at all remarkable. *Primo ballerino* good; *prima ballerina* good, and people say pretty, but I have not seen her near. There is a *grotesco* who jumps cleverly, but cannot write as I do – just as pigs grunt. The orchestra is tolerable. In Cremona, the orchestra is good, and Spagnoletta is the name of the first violinist there. *Prima donna* very passable – rather ancient, I fancy, and as ugly as sin. She does not sing as well as she acts, and is the wife of a violin-player at the opera. Her name is Masci. The opera was the 'Clemenza di

Tito'. *Seconda donna* not ugly on the stage, young, but nothing superior. *Primo uomo, un musico*, Cicognani, a fine voice, and a beautiful cantabile. The other two *musici* young and passable. The tenor's name is *non lo so* [I don't know what]. He has a pleasing exterior, and resembles Le Roi at Vienna. *Ballerino primo* good, but an ugly dog. There was a *ballerina* who danced far from badly, and, what is a *capo d' opera*, she is anything but plain, either on the stage or off it. The rest were the usual average. I cannot write much about the Milan opera, for we did not go there, but we heard that it was not successful. *Primo uomo*, Aprile, who sings well, and has a fine even voice; we heard him at a grand church festival. Madame Piccinelli, from Paris, who sang at one of our concerts, acts at the opera. Herr Pick, who danced at Vienna, is now dancing here. The opera is 'Didone abbandonata', but it is not to be given much longer. Signor Piccini, who is writing the next opera, is here. I am told that the title is to be 'Cesare in Egitto'.

Wolfgang de Mozart,
Noble of Hohenthal and attached to the Exchequer

Mozart to his Sister

Bologna, 24 March 1770

Oh, you busy creature!

Having been so long idle, I thought it would do me no harm to set to work again for a short time. On the post-days, when the German letters come, all that I eat and drink tastes better than usual. I beg you will let me know who are to sing in the oratorio, and also its title. Let me hear how you like the Haydn minuets, and whether they are better than the first. From my heart I rejoice to hear that Herr von Aman is now quite recovered; pray say to him that he must take great care of himself and beware of any unusual exertion. Be sure you tell him this. I intend shortly to send you a minuet that Herr Pick danced on the stage, and which every one in Milan was dancing at the *feste di ballo*, only that you may see by it how slowly people dance. The minuet itself is beautiful. Of course it comes from Vienna, so no doubt it is either Teller's or Starzer's. It has a great many notes. Why? Because it is a theatrical minuet, which is in slow time. The Milan and Italian minuets, however, have a vast number of notes, and are slow and with a quantity of bars; for instance, the first part has sixteen, the second twenty and even twenty-four.

We made the acquaintance of a singer in Parma, and also heard her to great advantage in her own house – I mean the far-famed Bastardella. She has, first, a fine voice; second, a flexible organ; third, an incredibly high compass . . .

Leopold Mozart to his Wife
Rome, 14 April 1770

... We arrived here safely on the 11th at noon. I could have been more easily persuaded to return to Salzburg than to proceed to Rome, for we had to travel for five days from Florence to Rome in the most dreadful rain and cold wind. I am told here that they have had constant rain for four months and indeed we had a sample of it, for we went on Wednesday and Thursday in fine weather to St. Peter's and to the Sistine Chapel to hear the Miserere during the Mass, and on our way home were surprised by such a frightful downpour that our cloaks have never yet been so soaked as they were then. But I will not give you a long description of that dreadful journey. Picture to yourself a more or less uncultivated country and the most horrible, filthy inns, where we got nothing to eat save here and there eggs and broccoli; while on fast-days they sometimes made a fuss about giving us the former. Fortunately we had a good supper at Viterbo and slept well. There we saw St. Rosa of Viterbo, whose body like that of St. Catherine at Bologna can be seen in a well-preserved condition. From the former saint we took away as a remembrance a fever antidote and relics, from the latter a belt. On arriving here on the 11th, we went to St. Peter's after lunch and then to Mass. On the 12th we were present at the Functiones, and when the Pope was serving the poor at table we were quite close to him, as we were standing beside him at the top of the table. This incident was all the more amazing as we had to pass through two doors guarded by Swiss guards in armour and make our way through many hundreds of people. And moreover you must note that we had as yet no acquaintances. But our fine clothes, the German tongue, and my usual freedom of manner which led me to make my servant order the Swiss guards in German to make way for us, soon helped us through everywhere. They took Wolfgang for a German courtier, while some even thought that he was a prince, which my servant allowed them to believe; I myself was taken for his tutor. Thus we made our way to the Cardinals' table. There Wolfgang happened to be standing between the chairs of two Cardinals, one of whom was Cardinal Pallavicini, who made a sign to him and said: '*Will you be so good as to tell me in confidence who you are?*' And Wolfgang told him. The Cardinal showed the greatest astonishment and said: '*Ah, you are the famous boy, about whom so many things have been written to me.*' Whereupon Wolfgang asked him: '*Are you not Cardinal Pallavicini?*' The Cardinal replied: '*Yes, I am, but why?*' Then Wolfgang told him *that we had letters to deliver to His Eminence and that we were going to pay him our respects.* The Cardinal appeared to be delighted, said that Wolfgang spoke Italian very well and among other things added: '*Ik kann auck ein benig deutsch sprecken.*' When we were leaving, Wolfgang kissed his hand and the Cardinal took off his berretta and bowed very politely. You have often heard of the famous Miserere in Rome, which is so greatly prized that the performers in the chapel are forbidden on pain of excommunication to take away a single part of it, to copy it or to give it to anyone. *But we have it already.* Wolfgang has written it down and we would have sent it to Salzburg in this letter, if it were not necessary for us to be there to perform it. But the manner of performance contributes more to its effect than the composition itself. So we shall bring it home with us. Moreover, as it is one of the secrets of Rome, we do not wish to let it fall into other hands, *ut non incurramus mediate vel immediate in censuram Ecclesiae ...*

Mozart to his Mother and Sister
(a postscript to his father's letter)
Rome, 14 April 1770

I am thankful to say that my stupid pen and I are all right, so we send a thousand kisses to you both. I wish that my sister were in Rome, for this city would assuredly delight her, because St. Peter's is symmetrical, and many other things in Rome are also symmetrical. Papa has just told me that the loveliest flowers are being carried past at this moment. That I am no wiseacre is pretty well known. Oh! I have one annoyance – there is only a single bed in our lodgings, so mamma may easily imagine that I get no rest beside papa. I rejoice at the thoughts of a new lodging. I have just finished sketching St. Peter with his keys, St. Paul with his sword, and St. Luke with – my sister, &c., &c. I had the honour of kissing St. Peter's foot at San Pietro, and as I have the misfortune to be so short your good old

Wolfgang Mozart
was lifted up!

Leopold Mozart to his Wife
Rome, 21 April 1770

... In Florence we came across a young Englishman, who is a pupil of the famous violinist Nardini. This boy [Thomas Linley], who *plays most beautifully* and who is the same age and the same size as Wolfgang, came to the house of the learned poetess, Signora Corilla, where we happened to be on the introduction of M. De L'Augier. The two boys performed one after the other throughout the whole evening, constantly embracing each other. On the following day the little Englishman, a most charming boy, had his violin brought to our rooms and played the whole afternoon, Wolfgang accompanying him on his own. On the next day we lunched with M. Gavard, the administrator of the grand ducal finances, and these two boys played in turn the whole afternoon, not like boys, but like men! Little

Tommaso accompanied us home and wept bitter tears, because we were leaving on the following day. But when he heard that our departure would not take place until noon, he called on us at nine o'clock in the morning and gave Wolfgang with many embraces the following poem, which Signora Corilla had to compose for him on the previous evening. Then he accompanied our carriage as far as the city gate. I wish you had witnessed this scene . . .

Mozart to his Sister
Rome, mistress of the world: 25 April 1770

Dearest Sister,

I assure you that I always expect with intense eagerness my letters from Salzburg on post-days. Yesterday we were at S. Lorenzo and heard vespers, and today at the chanted mass, and in the evening at the second vespers, because it was the Feast of the Madonna del Buonconsiglio. A few days ago we were at the Campidoglio, where we saw a great many fine things. If I tried to write you an account of all I saw, this sheet would not suffice. I played at two concerts, and tomorrow I am to play at another. After dinner we played at Potsch [Boccia]. This is a game I have learnt, and when I come home I will teach it to you. When I have finished this letter, I am going to complete a symphony that I have begun. The aria is finished. The copyist (who is my father) has the symphony, because we do not choose it to be copied by any one else, or it might be stolen.

Wolfgango in Germany
Amadeo Mozart in Italy

Mozart to his Mother and Sister
(a postscript to a letter of his father's)
Rome, 2 May 1770

Praise and thanks be to God, I am well and kiss Mamma's hand and my sister's face, nose, mouth, neck and my bad pen and arse, if it is clean.

Wolfgango Mozart

Leopold Mozart to his Wife
Naples, 19 May 1770

... We drove yesterday to Portici to call on the minister, Marchese Tanucci, and we shall drive out there again tomorrow. We had dreadful roads and a very cool breeze. We have left our fine cloth suits in Rome and have had to put on our two beautifully braided summer costumes. Wolfgang's is of rose-coloured moiré, but the colour is so peculiar that in Italy it is called colore di fuoco or flame-coloured; it is trimmed with silver lace and lined with sky-blue silk. My costume is cinnamon-coloured and made of piquéd Florentine cloth with silver lace and lined with apple green silk. They are two fine costumes, but, before we reach home, they will look like old maids. Yesterday evening we called on the English ambassador, Hamilton, a London acquaintance of ours, whose wife plays the clavier with unusual feeling and is a very pleasant person. She trembled at having to play before Wolfgang. She has a valuable instrument, made in England by Tschudi, which has two manuals and a pedal, so that the two manuals can be disconnected by the action of the foot. We found at Hamilton's house Mr. Beckford and Mr. Weis, also London acquaintances. We lunched on the 16th with Tschudi, who had been in Salzburg and requested me to convey his greetings to Count Spaur and to all his good friends and very many compliments to you especially and to Nannerl. He embraced us constantly, particularly on our arrival and departure, and offered us his services on all occasions ...

On reading the article about the Miserere, we simply burst out laughing. There is not the slightest cause for anxiety. Everywhere else far more fuss is being made about Wolfgang's feat. All Rome knows, even the Pope himself, that he wrote it down. There is nothing whatever to fear; on the contrary, the achievement has done him great credit, as you will shortly hear. You will see to it that the letter is read out everywhere, so that we may be sure that His Grace hears what Wolfgang has done. If the portraits are good likenesses, you may pay the painter whatever you like.

Now I must close, for we are off to the Imperial Ambassador the Count von Kaunitz. Farewell, we kiss you and Nannerl 1000 times and

I am your old

MZT

I trust that your cold left you long ago.

Mozart to his Sister

Naples, 5 June 1770

Vesuvius is smoking fiercely! Thunder and lightning and blazes! *Haid homa gfresa beim Herr Doll. Das is a deutscha Compositor, und a browa Mo.** Now I begin to describe my course of life — *Alle 9 ore, qualche volta anche alle dieci mi svelgio, e poi andiamo fuor di casa, e poi pranzi-amo da un trattore, e dopo pranzo scriviamo, e poi sortiamo, e indi ceniamo, ma che cosa? Al giorno di grasso, un mezzo pollo ovvero un piccolo boccone d' arrosto; al giorno di magro un piccolo pesce; e di poi andiamo a dormire. Est-ce que vous avez compris? — Redma dafir Soisburgarisch, don as is gschaida. Wir sand Gottlob gesund da Voda und i.*** I hope

---

* 'Today we dined with Herr Doll; he is a good composer and a worthy man.' [Vienna *Patois.*]

** 'I rise generally every morning at 9 o'clock, but sometimes not till 10, when we go out. We dine at a restaurateur's; after dinner I write, and then we go out again, and afterwards sup, but on what? on *jours gras*, half a fowl, or a small slice of roast meat; on *jours maigres*, a little fish, and then we go to sleep. Do you understand? Let us talk Salzburgisch, for that is more sensible. Thank God, my father and I are well.' [*Patois.*]

38

you and mamma are so also. Naples and Rome are two drowsy cities. *A scheni Schrift! net wor?** Write to me, and do not be so lazy. *Altrimente avrete qualche bastonate di me. Quel plaisir! Je te casserai la tête.*** I am delighted with the thoughts of the portraits [of his mother and sister, who had promised to have their likenesses taken], *und i bi korios wias da gleich sieht; wons ma gfoin, so los i mi und den Vodan a so macho. Maidli, lass Da saga, wo bist dan gwesa he?*+ The opera here is Jomelli's; it is fine, but too grave and old-fashioned for this stage. Madame de' Amicis sings incomparably, and so does Aprile, who used to sing at Milan. The dancing is miserably pretentious. The theatre beautiful. The King has been brought up in the rough Neapolitan fashion, and at the opera always stands on a stool, so that he may look a little taller than the Queen, who is beautiful and so gracious, for she bowed to me in the most condescending manner no less than six times on the Molo.

Leopold Mozart to his Wife
Rome, 4 July 1770

... This very moment a servant of Cardinal Pallavicini

* 'Fine writing, is it not?' [*Patois.*]
** 'Otherwise I will cudgel you soundly. What a pleasure – to break your head!'
+ 'And I am anxious to see what they are like, and then I will have my father and myself also taken. Fair maiden, say, where have you been, eh?' [*Patois.*]

has invited us to lunch with His Eminence tomorrow. We are dining on Friday with His Excellency the Tuscan Ambassador, Baron Sant' Odile. Tomorrow we are to hear a piece of news which, if it is true, will fill you both with amazement. For Cardinal Pallavicini is said to have been commanded by the Pope to hand Wolfgang the cross and diploma of an order.* Do not speak much about this yet. If it is true, I shall write to you next Saturday. When we were at the Cardinal's house a few days ago he once or twice called Wolfgang 'Signor Cavaliere'. We thought that he was joking, but now I hear it is true and that this is behind tomorrow's invitation. Addio! Farewell! I must hurry, for the post is going. Wolfgang cannot send you a letter, as he is writing to the son of Field-marshal Pallavicini in Bologna. We kiss you 1000 times.

MZT

Wolfgang grew noticeably in Naples.

Leopold Mozart to his Wife
Rome, 7 July 1770

... What I wrote the other day about the cross of an order is quite correct. It is the same order as Gluck's and is worded as follows: *te creamus auratae militiae*

---

* The Order of the Golden Spur, which Pope Clement XIV conferred on Mozart on 8 July 1770.

equitem. Wolfgang has to wear a beautiful gold cross, which he has received. You can imagine how I laugh when I hear people calling him 'Signor Cavaliere' all the time. Tomorrow we are to have an audience with the Pope ...

Mozart to his Sister (a postscript to his father's letter)
Rome, 7 July 1770

Cara Sorrella Mia!

I am really surprised that you can compose so charmingly. In a word, the song is beautiful. Often try something similar. Send me soon the other six minuets of Haydn. *Mademoiselle, j'ai l'honneur d'être votre très-humble serviteur et frère,*

Chevalier de Mozart

Mozart to his Sister
(a postscript to a letter of his father's)
Bologna, 4 August 1770

I grieve from my heart to hear that Jungfrau Marthe is still so ill, and I pray every day that she may recover. Tell her from me that she must beware of much fatigue and eat only what is strongly salted [she was consumptive]. *A propos*, did you give my letter to Robinsiegerl? [Sigismund Robinig, a friend of his]. You did not mention it when you wrote. I beg that when you see

41

him you will tell him he is not quite to forget me. I can't possibly write better, for my pen is only fit to write music and not a letter. My violin has been newly strung, and I play every day. I only mention this because mamma wished to know whether I still played the violin. I have had the honour to go at least six times by myself into the churches to attend their splendid ceremonies. In the meantime I have composed four Italian symphonies [overtures], besides five or six arias, and also a motett.

Does Herr Deibl often come to see you? Does he still honour you by his amusing conversation? And the noble Herr Carl von Vogt, does he still deign to listen to your tiresome voices? Herr von Schiedenhofen must assist you often in writing minuets, otherwise he shall have no sugar-plums.

If time permitted, it would be my duty to trouble Herr von Mölk and Herr von Schiedenhofen with a few lines; but as that most indispensable of all things is wanting, I hope they will forgive my neglect, and consider me henceforth absolved from this honour. I have begun various cassations [a kind of divertimento], so I have thus responded to your desire. I don't think the piece in question can be one of mine, for who would venture to publish as his own composition what is, in reality, written by the son of the Capellmeister, and whose mother and sister are in the same town?

Addio – farewell! My sole recreations consist in dancing English hornpipes and cutting capers. Italy is a land of sleep; I am always drowsy here. Addio – goodbye!

Mozart to his Mother and Sister
(a postscript to a letter of his father's)
Bologna, 21 August 1770

I am not only still alive, but in capital spirits. Today I took a fancy to ride a donkey, for such is the custom in Italy, so I thought that I too must give it a trial. We have the honour to associate with a certain Dominican who is considered a very pious ascetic. I somehow don't quite think so, for he constantly takes a cup of chocolate for breakfast, and immediately afterwards a large glass of strong Spanish wine; and I have myself had the privilege of dining with this holy man, when he drank a lot of wine at dinner and a full glass of very strong wine afterwards, two large slices of melons, some peaches and pears for dessert, five cups of coffee, a whole plateful of nuts, and two dishes of milk and lemons. This he may perhaps do out of bravado, but I don't think so – at all events, it is far too much; and he eats a great deal also at his afternoon collation.

Mozart to Thomas Linley, Florence
Bologna, 10 September 1770

My Dear Friend,

Here is a letter at last! Indeed I am very late in replying to your charming letter addressed to me at Naples,
which, however, I only received two months after you
had written it. My father's plan was to travel to Loreto
via Bologna, and thence to Milan via Florence, Leghorn
and Genoa. We should then have given you a surprise
by turning up unexpectedly in Florence. But, as he had
the misfortune to gash his leg rather badly when the
shaft-horse of our carriage fell on the road, and as this
wound not only kept him in bed for three weeks but
held us up in Bologna for another seven, this nasty accident has forced us to change our plans and to proceed
to Milan via Parma.

First, we have missed the suitable time for such a
journey and, second, the season is over, for everyone
is in the country and therefore we could not earn our
expenses. I assure you that this accident has annoyed
us very much. I would do everything in my power to
have the pleasure of embracing my dear friend. Moreover my father and I would very much like to meet again
Signor Gavard and his very dear and charming family,
and also Signora Corilla and Signor Nardini, and then
to return to Bologna. This we would do indeed, if we

had the slightest hope of recouping even the expenses of our journey.

As for the engravings you lost, my father remembered you; and his order arrived in time for two other copies to be kept for you. So please let me know of some means of sending them to you. Keep me in your friendship and believe that my affection for you will endure for ever and that I am your most devoted servant and loving friend

Amadeo Wolfgango Mozart

Mozart to his Mother
(a postscript to a letter of his father's)
Milan, 20 October 1770

My dear Mamma,

I cannot write much, for my fingers ache from writing out such a quantity of recitative. I hope you will pray for me that my opera ['Mitridate Rè di Ponto'] may go off well, and that we soon may have a joyful meeting. I kiss your hands a thousand times, and have a great deal to say to my sister; but what? That is known only to God and myself. Please God, I hope soon to be able to confide it to her verbally; in the meantime, I send her a thousand kisses. My compliments to all kind friends. We have lost our good Martherl, but we hope that by the mercy of God she is now in a state of blessedness.

Leopold Mozart to his Wife
Milan, 22 December 1770

... Picture to yourselves little Wolfgang in a scarlet suit, trimmed with gold braid and lined with sky-blue satin. The tailor is starting to make it today. Wolfgang will wear this suit during the first three days when he is seated at the clavier. The one which was made for him in Salzburg is too short by half a foot and in any case is too tight and too small ...

Mozart to his Sister
(a postscript to a letter of his father's)
Milan, 12 January 1771

My darling Sister,

It is long since I have written to you, having been so much occupied with my opera. As I have now more time, I shall attend better to my duty. My opera, thank God, is popular, as the theatre is full every evening, which causes great surprise, for many say that during all the time they have lived in Milan they never saw any first opera so crowded as on this occasion. I am thankful to say that both papa and I are quite well, and I hope at Easter to have an opportunity of relating everything to mamma and you. Addio! *A propos*, the copyist was with us yesterday, and said that he was at that moment engaged in transcribing my opera for the Lisbon court. Goodbye, my dear Madlle. sister,

Always and ever your attached brother.

Mozart and his father returned to Salzburg in March 1771, but the success of Mitridate *in Milan had been so great that the young composer was invited to return later in the same year, and was asked back yet again to produce an opera,* Lucio Silla, *for the carnival season of 1772–3.*

Leopold Mozart to his Wife
Milan, 18 December 1772

... I am writing this letter today, Friday the 18th, for tomorrow we shall hardly have time to write anything, because we are to have the first rehearsal with all the instruments at half past nine in the morning. During the last few days we have had three rehearsals of the recitatives. The tenor arrived only yesterday evening and today Wolfgang composed two arias for him and has still two more to do. The second rehearsal takes place on Sunday the 20th, the third on Tuesday the 22nd, and the dress rehearsal on Wednesday the 23rd. On Thursday and Friday there will be no rehearsals; but on Saturday the 26th, the very day on which you will receive this letter, we shall have the first performance of the opera. I am writing to you at eleven o'clock at night and Wolfgang has just finished the second aria for the tenor. We shall celebrate Christmas Eve at supper with Herr and Frau von Germani, who send you greetings and wish that you were here. We are lunching tomorrow with Herr von Mayr and after lunch I shall still be able to write a few words. Addio. Farewell.

Mozart to his Sister
(a postscript to his father's letter)
Milan, 18 December 1772

I hope, dear sister, that you are well, dear sister. When this letter reaches you, dear sister, my opera will be *in scena*, dear sister. Think of me, dear sister, and try, dear sister, to imagine with all your might that my dear sister sees and hears it also. In truth, it is hard to say, as it is now eleven o'clock at night, but I do believe, and don't at all doubt, that in the daytime it is brighter than at Easter. My dear sister, tomorrow we dine with Herr von Mayer; and do you know why? Guess! Because he invited us. The rehearsal tomorrow is to be in the theatre. The *impresario*, Signor Cassiglioni, has entreated me not to say a word of this to a soul, as all kinds of people would come crowding in, and that we don't wish. So, my child, I beg, my child, that you won't say one syllable to any one on the subject, or too many people would come crowding in, my child. *Approposito*, do you know the history that occurred here? Well, I will relate it to you. We were going home straight from Count Firmiani's, and when we came into our street we opened our door, and what do you think happened? We went in. Goodbye, my pet. Your unworthy brother (frater),

Wolfgang

In the summer of 1773 father and son spent two months in Vienna in the hope of obtaining a court appointment for Wolfgang. They had no success, and after a period in Salzburg the young composer accepted a commission for an opera buffa, La finta giardiniera, *in Munich, where he arrived with his father early in December 1774. By now his considerable experience of life in more stimulating foreign cities was making him increasingly aware of the limitations of his Salzburg existence.*

Mozart to his Mother
Munich, 14 January 1775

God be praised! My opera was given yesterday, the 13th, and proved so successful that I cannot possibly describe all the tumult. In the first place, the whole theatre was so crammed that many people were obliged to go away. After each aria there was invariably a tremendous uproar and clapping of hands, and cries of *Viva Maestro!* Her Serene Highness the Electress and the Dowager (who were opposite me) also called out Bravo! When the opera was over, during the interval when all is usually quiet till the ballet begins, the applause and shouts of *Bravo!* were renewed; sometimes there was a lull, but only to recommence afresh, and so forth. I afterwards went with papa to a room through which the Elector and the whole court were to pass. I kissed the hands of the Elector and the Electress and the other royalties, who were all very gracious. At an early hour this morning the Prince Bishop of Chiemsee [who had most probably procured the *scrittura* for his young friend Wolfgang] sent to congratulate me that the opera had proved such a brilliant success in every respect. As to our return home, it is not likely to be soon, nor should mamma wish it, for she must know well what a good thing it is to have a little breathing-time. We shall come quite soon enough to ———. One most just and undeniable reason is, that my opera is to be given again on Friday next, and I am very necessary at the performance, or it might be difficult to recognise it again. There are very odd ways here. 1,000 kisses to Miss Bimberl [the dog].

Mozart to Padre Martini, Bologna
Salzburg, 4 September 1776

Most reverend and esteemed Father and Maestro,

The veneration, the esteem, and the respect I feel for your illustrious person, induce me to intrude on you with this letter, and also to send you a small portion of my music, which I venture to submit to your masterly judgment. [Last year, at Monaco in Bavaria, I wrote an opera buffa ('La finta Giardiniera') for the Carnival. A few days previous to my departure from thence, his Electoral Highness wished to hear some of my contrapuntal music; I was therefore obliged to write this motett in haste, to allow time for the score to be copied for his Highness, and to arrange the parts so that it might be produced on the following Sunday at grand mass at the offertory. Most dear and highly esteemed Maestro, I do entreat you to give me unreservedly your candid opinion of the motett. We live in this world in order always to learn industriously, and to enlighten each other by means of discussion and to strive vigorously to promote the progress of science and the fine arts. Oh, how many and many a time have I desired to be nearer you, that I might converse and discuss with your Reverence! I live in a country where music has very little success [though, exclusive of those who have forsaken us, we have still admirable professors, and more particularly composers of great solidity, knowledge, and taste.] We are rather badly off at the theatre from the want of actors. We have no *musici*, nor shall we find it very easy to get any, because they insist upon being well paid; and generosity is not a failing of ours. I amuse myself in the meantime by writing church and chamber music; and we have two excellent contrapuntists here, Haydn and Adlgasser. My father is maestro at the Metropolitan church, which gives me an opportunity to write for the church as much as I please. Moreover, my father has been thirty-six years in the service of this court, and knowing that our present Archbishop neither can nor will endure the sight of elderly people, he does not take it to heart, but devotes himself to literature, which was always his favourite pursuit. Our church music is rather different from that of Italy, and the more so, as a mass including the *Kyrie, Gloria, Credo,* the *Sonata all' Epistola,* the *Offertory* or *Motett, Sanctus,* and *Agnus Dei,* and even a solemn mass, when the Prince himself officiates, must never last more than three-quarters of an hour. A particular course of study is required for this class of composition. And what must such a mass be, scored with all the instruments, war-drums, cymbals, &c., &c.! Oh! why are we so far apart, dearest Signor Maestro? for how many things I have to say to you! I devoutly revere all the *Signori Filarmonici.* I venture to recommend myself to your good opinion; I shall never cease regretting being so distant from the person in the world whom I most love, venerate, and esteem. I beg to subscribe myself, reverend Father, always your most humble and devoted servant,

Wolfgang Amadeus Mozart

In August 1777, Mozart wrote to the Archbishop of Salzburg, asking to be discharged from his service. A note from the Archbishop to his Court Chamberlain on 28 August 1777 communicated his decision that 'in the name of the Gospel father and son have my permission to seek their fortune elsewhere'. Leopold Mozart in fact stayed on in his Court appointment, but in less than a month Wolfgang was off again, this time with his mother only, on what was intended to be a tour of the musical centres of southern Germany in search of a permanent job. After a couple of unfruitful weeks in Munich they moved on to Augsburg (Leopold's birthplace) and thence to Mannheim where they stayed for four and a half months. In spite of the many new friends he made there, and the stimulation provided by the artistic life of one of the liveliest musical cities in Europe, Mozart made no headway in his attempts to get a Court appointment. As his financial situation became more and more precarious, it became clear that the tour of southern Germany had to be abandoned in favour of something more radical.

Mozart to his Father
Munich, 26 September 1777

We arrived safely in Munich on the afternoon of the 24th, at half-past four o'clock. A complete novelty to me was being obliged to drive to the Custom House, escorted by a grenadier with a fixed bayonet. The first person we knew, who met us when driving, was Signor Consoli; he recognised me at once, and showed the utmost joy at seeing me again. Next day he called on us. I cannot attempt to describe the delight of Herr Albert [the 'learned landlord' of the Black Eagle, on the Kaufinger Gasse, now Hôtel Detzer]; he is indeed a truly honest man, and a very good friend of ours. On my arrival I went to the piano, and did not leave it till

dinner-time. Herr Albert was not at home, but he soon
came in, and we went down to dinner together. There
I met M. Sfeer and a certain secretary, an intimate friend
of his; both send their compliments to you. Though
tired by our journey, we did not go to bed till late; we,
however, rose next morning at seven o'clock. My hair
was in such disorder that I could not go to Count
Seeau's till half-past ten o'clock. When I got there I was
told that he had driven out to the *chasse*. Patience! In the
meantime, I wished to call on Chorus-master Bernard,
but he had gone to the country with Baron Schmid.
I found Herr von Belvall deeply engaged in business; he
sent you a thousand compliments. Rossi came to dinner,
and at two o'clock Consoli, and at three arrived Becke
[a friend of Mozart's and an admirable flute-player],
and also Herr von Bellvall. I paid a visit to Frau von
Durst [with whom Nannerl had lived], who now lodges
with the Franciscans. At six o'clock I took a short walk
with Herr Becke. There is a Professor Huber here,
whom you may perhaps remember better than I do; he
says that the last time he either saw or heard me was
at Vienna, at Herr von Mesmer's, junior. He is neither
tall nor short, pale, with silvery-grey hair, and his
physiognomy rather like that of Herr Unterbereiter.
This gentleman is vice-intendant of the theatre; his
occupation is to read through all the comedies to be
acted, to improve or to spoil, to add to or to put them
aside. He comes every evening to Albert's, and often

talks to me. Today, Friday, the 26th, I called on Count Seeau at half-past eight o'clock. This was what passed. As I was going into the house I met Madame Niesser, the actress, just coming out, who said, 'I suppose you wish to see the Count?' 'Yes!' 'He is still in his garden, and Heaven knows when he may come!' I asked her where the garden was. 'As I must see him also,' said she, 'let us go together.' We had scarcely left the house when we saw the Count coming towards us about twelve paces off; he recognised and instantly named me. He was very polite, and seemed already to know all that had taken place about me. We went up the steps together slowly and alone; I told him briefly the whole affair. He said that I ought at once to request an audience of his Highness the Elector, but that, if I failed in obtaining it, I must make a written statement. I entreated him to keep this all quite private, and he agreed to do so. When I remarked to him that there really was room for a genuine composer here, he said, 'I know that well.' I afterwards went to the Bishop of Chiemsee, and was with him for half an hour. I told him everything, and he promised to do all he could for me in the matter. At one o'clock he drove to Nymphenburg, and declared positively he would speak to the Electress. On Sunday the Count comes here. Herr Joannes Krönner has been appointed Vice-Concertmeister, which he owes to a blunt speech of his. He has produced two symphonies – *Deo mene liberi* [God preserve me from such] – of his own composition. The Elector asked him, 'Did you really compose these?' 'Yes, your Royal Highness!' 'From whom did you learn?' 'From a schoolmaster in Switzerland, where so much importance is attached to the study of composition. This schoolmaster taught me more than all your composers here, put together, could teach me.' Count Schönborn and his Countess, a sister of the Archbishop [of Salzburg], passed through here today. I chanced to be at the play at the time. Herr Albert, in the course of conversation, told them that I was here, and that I had given up my situation. They were all astonishment, and positively refused to believe him when he said that my salary, of blessed memory, was only twelve florins thirty kreuzers! They merely changed horses, and would gladly have spoken with me, but I was too late to meet them. Now I must enquire what you are doing, and how you are. Mamma and I hope that you are quite well. I am still in my very happiest humour; my head feels as light as a feather since I got away from that chicanery. I have grown fatter already.

Mozart to his Father
Munich, 29–30 September 1777

True enough, a great many kind friends, but unluckily most of them have little or nothing in their power. I was with Count Seeau yesterday, at half-past ten o'clock, and found him graver and less natural than the first time; but it was only in appearance, for today I was at Prince Zeill's [Bishop of Chiemsee], who, with all courtesy, said to me, 'I don't think we shall effect much here. During dinner, at Nymphenburg, I spoke privately to the Elector, who replied: "It is too soon at this moment; he must leave this and go to Italy aud become famous. I do not actually reject him, but these are too early days as yet."' There it is! Most of these grandees have such paroxysms of enthusiasm for Italy. Still, he advised me to go to the Elector, and to place my case before him as I had previously intended. I spoke confidentially at dinner today with Herr Woschitka [violoncellist in the Munich court orchestra, and a member of the Elector's private band], and he appointed me to come tomorrow at nine o'clock, when he will certainly procure me an audience. We are very good friends now. He insisted on knowing the name of my informant; but I said to him, 'Rest assured that I am your friend and shall continue to be so; I am in turn equally convinced of your friend-ship, so you must be satisfied with this.' But to return to my narrative. The Bishop of Chiemsee also spoke to the Electress when *tête-à-tête* with her. She shrugged her shoulders, and said she would do her best, but was very doubtful as to her success. I now return to Count Seeau, who asked Prince Zeill (after he had told him everything), 'Do you know whether Mozart has not enough from his family to entice him to remain here

with a little assistance? I should really like to keep him.'
Prince Zeill answered: 'I don't know, but I doubt it
much; all you have to do is to speak to himself on the
subject.' This, then, was the cause of Count Seeau being
so thoughtful on the following day. I like being here,
and I am of the same opinion with many of my friends,
that if I could only remain here for a year or two I might
acquire both money and fame by my works, and then
more probably be sought by the court than be obliged
to seek it myself. Since my return here Herr Albert has
a project in his head, the fulfilment of which does not
seem to me impossible. It is this: He wishes to form an
association of ten kind friends, each of these to subscribe
1 ducat (50 gulden) monthly, 600 florins a year. If in
addition to this I had even 200 florins per annum from
Count Seeau, this would make 800 florins altogether.
How does papa like this idea? Is it not friendly? Ought
not I to accept it if they are in earnest? I am perfectly
satisfied with it; for I should be near Salzburg, and
if you, dearest papa, were seized with a fancy to leave
Salzburg (which from my heart I wish you were) and to
pass your life in Munich, how easy and pleasant would
it be! For if we are obliged to live in Salzburg with 504
florins, surely we might live in Munich with 800?

Today, the 30th, after a conversation with Herr
Woschitka, I went to court by appointment. Every one
was in hunting costume. Baron Kern was the chamberlain on service. I might have gone there last night, but

I could not offend M. Woschitka, who himself offered to find me an opportunity of speaking to the Elector. At 10 o'clock he took me into a narrow little room, through which his Royal Highness was to pass on his way to hear mass, before going to hunt. Count Seeau went by, and greeted me very kindly: 'How are you, dear Mozart?' When the Elector came up to me, I said, 'Will your Royal Highness permit me to pay my homage and to offer your Royal Highness my services?' 'So you have finally left Salzburg?' 'I have left it for ever, your Royal Highness. I only asked leave to make a journey, and being refused I was obliged to take this step, although I have long intended to leave Salzburg, which is no place for me, I feel sure.' 'Good heavens! you are quite a young man. But your father is still in Salzburg?' 'Yes, your Royal Highness; he humbly lays his homage at your feet, &c., &c. I have already been three times in Italy. I have written three operas, and am a member of the Bologna Academy; I underwent a trial where several *maestri* toiled and laboured for four or five hours, whereas I finished my work in one. This is a sufficient testimony that I have abilities to serve any court. My greatest wish is to be appointed by your Royal Highness, who is himself such a great &c., &c.' 'But, my good young friend, I regret that there is not a single vacancy. If there were only a vacancy!' 'I can assure your Royal Highness that I would do credit to Munich.' 'Yes, but what does that avail when there is no vacancy?' This he said as he was moving on; so I bowed and took leave of his Royal Highness. Herr Woschitka advises me to place myself often in the way of the Elector. This afternoon I went to Count Salern's. His daughter is a maid of honour, and was one of the hunting party. Ravani and I were in the street when the whole procession passed. The Elector and the Electress noticed me very kindly. Young Countess Salern recognised me at once, and waved her hand to me repeatedly. Baron Rumling, whom I had previously seen in the antechamber, never was so courteous to me as on this occasion. I will soon write to you what passed with Salern. He was very kind, polite, and straightforward. – P.S. Ma très-chère sœur, next time I mean to write you a letter all for yourself. My remembrances to B. C. M. R. and various other letters of the alphabet. Adieu! A man built a house here and inscribed on it: 'Building is beyond all doubt an immense pleasure, but I little thought that it would cost so much treasure.' During the night some one wrote underneath, 'You ought first to have counted the cost.'

Maria Anna Mozart to her Husband
Munich, 2–3 October 1777

Wolfgang is lunching today with Madame Branca and I have lunched at home; but at three o'clock I am going to Frau von Tosson, who is sending someone to fetch me. Herr von Krimmel turned up again yesterday with

Herr von Unhold. He is a good friend of ours and is trying hard to persuade us to go to Memmingen and to give a first-class concert, as he assures us that we shall make more there than at a court. I quite believe it, for, as hardly anybody goes to such a place, the people there are glad when they can get anyone at all. Now how is your health? I am not really satisfied with your letters. I don't like that cough, which is lasting far too long. You ought not to have anything wrong with you at all. I beg you to use the sago soon, and the sooner the better, so that you may regain your strength as quickly as possible. We received the parcel by the mail coach and the other one too by the ordinary post. I send greetings to Nannerl. Please tell her not to get cross with you and to take good care that you have no worries and to help you to pass the time so that you do not get melancholy. Bimperl, I trust, is doing her duty and making up to you, for she is a good and faithful fox terrier. I send greetings to Tresel also and should like you to tell her that it is all one whether

Mozart continues

[I shit the dirt or she eats it. But now for something more sensible ...] At four o'clock I went to Frau von Tosson, where I found Mamma and Frau von Hepp. I played there until eight o'clock and then we went home. About half past nine in the evening a small

61

orchestra of five players, two clarinets, two horns and one bassoon, came up to the house. Herr Albert (whose name-day is tomorrow) had ordered this music in his and my honour. They did not play at all badly together. They were the same people who play in Albert's dining-hall during the meals. But you can tell at once that Fiala has trained them. They played some of his compositions and I must say that they were very pretty and that he has some very good ideas.

Tomorrow we are going to have a little scratch-concert among ourselves, but, I should add, on that wretched clavier. Oh! Oh! Oh! Well, I wish you a very restful night and I improve on this good wish by hearing to hope soon that Papa is well quite. I forgiveness your crave for my disgraceful handwriting, but ink, haste, sleep, dreams and all the rest ... I Papa your, my hands kiss, a thousand times dearest, and my embrace, the heart, sister I with all my brute of a, and remain, now and for ever, amen,

Wolfgang most obedient your
Amadé Mozart son

Leopold Mozart to his Son
Salzburg, 4 October 1777

Mon très cher Fils!

I have no great hopes of anything happening in Munich. Unless there is a vacancy, the Elector is bound to refuse to take anyone and, moreover, there are always secret enemies about, whose fears would prevent your getting an appointment. Herr Albert's scheme is indeed a proof of the greatest friendship imaginable. Yet, however possible it may seem to you to find ten persons, each of whom will give you a ducat a month, to me it is quite inconceivable. For who are these philanthropists or these music-lovers? And what sort of undertaking or service will they require from you in return? To me it seems far more likely that Count Seeau may contribute something. But unless he does, what you may expect from Albert would be no more than a trifle. If he could make the arrangement even for a year – that is all I will say for the moment – then you could accept an offer from Count Seeau. But what would he demand! – perhaps all the work which Herr Michl has been doing? Running about and training singers! That would be a dog's life and quite out of the question! In short, I cannot see where these ten delightful friends are to come from. Further, Albert may not be able to see them at once, as some of them are perhaps out of town. Moreover, I should prefer merchants or other honest persons to these courtiers, for a great deal would depend on whether they would keep their word and for how long. *If the arrangement is immediately practicable, well and good, and you ought to accept it.* But if it cannot be made at once, then you simply must not lounge about, use up your money and waste your time. For in spite of all the compliments and shows of friendship which you are receiving, you cannot hope to make a farthing in Munich! ...

... I have just been to see the Chief Steward, who is paying me a special visit one day in order that I may tell him everything in detail. For there is no peace at his house; someone is always being announced or else his Countess comes rushing in. He loves you with his whole heart. Before he heard our story, he had already bought four horses and was looking forward to the pleasure he would give you by turning up with one of them for you to ride on. When, however, he heard about our trouble, he simply could not express his annoyance. He was paying his respects one day to the Archbishop, who said to him: '*Now we have one man less in the orchestra.*' Firmian replied: '*Your Grace has lost a great virtuoso.*' '*Why?*' asked the Prince. The reply was: '*Mozart is the greatest player on the clavier whom I have ever heard in my life; on the violin he rendered very good services to Your Grace; and he is a first-rate composer.*' The Archbishop was silent, for he had nothing to say. Now I must close because I have no more room. When writing you should at least mention *whether you have had such and such a letter*. You must surely have received by now the parcel containing the roll with the diplomas and Padre Martini's testimonial. We kiss you millions of times and I am your old

Mozart

Be careful not to lose Padre Martini's testimonial.

Mozart to his Father

Munich, 11 October 1777

Why have I not as yet written anything about Misliweczeck? Because I was only too glad not to think of
him; for when he is spoken of I invariably hear how
highly he praises me, and what a kind and true friend
he is of mine; but then follow pity and lamentation. He
was described to me, and deeply was I distressed. How
could I bear that Misliweczeck, my intimate friend,
should be in the same town, nay, even in the same corner
of the world with me, and neither see him nor speak to
him? Impossible! so I resolved to go to visit him. On
the previous day, I called on the manager of the Duke's
Hospital to ask if I might see my friend in the garden,
which I thought best, though the doctors assured me
there was no longer any risk of infection. The manager
agreed to my proposal, and said I should find him in the
garden between eleven and twelve o'clock, and, if he
was not there when I came, to send for him. Next day
I went with Herr von Hamm, secretary in the Crown
Office (of whom I shall speak presently), and mamma to
the Duke's Hospital. Mamma went into the Hospital
church, and we into the garden. Misliweczeck was not
there, so we sent him a message. I saw him coming
across, and knew him at once from his manner of
walking. I must tell you that he had already sent me his
remembrances by Herr Heller, a violoncello-player, and

begged me to visit him before I left Munich. When he came up to me, we shook hands cordially. 'You see,' said he, 'how unfortunate I am.' These words and his appearance, which papa is already aware of from description, so went to my heart that I could only say, with tears in my eyes, 'I pity you from my heart, my dear friend.' He saw how deeply I was affected, so rejoined quite cheerfully, 'Now tell me what you are doing; when I heard that you were in Munich, I could scarcely believe it; how could Mozart be here and not long ago have come to see me?' 'I hope you will forgive me, but I had such a number of visits to make, and I have so many kind friends here.' 'I feel quite sure that you have indeed many kind friends, but a truer friend than myself you cannot have.' He asked me whether papa had told me anything of a letter he had received. I said, 'Yes, he did write to me (I was quite confused, and trembled so much in every limb that I could scarcely speak), but he gave me no details.' He then told me that Signor Gaetano Santoro, the Neapolitan *impresario*, was obliged, owing to *impegni* and *protezione*, to give the composition of the opera for this Carnival to a certain Maestro Valentini; but he added, 'Next year he has three at liberty, one of which is to be at my service. But as I have already composed six times for Naples, I don't in the least mind undertaking the less promising one, and making over to you the best libretto, viz, the one for the Carnival. God knows whether I shall be able to travel by that time, but if not, I shall send back the *scrittura*. The company for next year is good, being all people whom I have recommended. You must know that I have such influence in Naples that, when I say engage such a one, they do so at once.' *Marquesi* is the *primo uomo*, whom he, and indeed all Munich too, praises very highly; Marchiani is a good *prima donna*, and there is a tenor, whose name I cannot recall, but Misliweczeck says he is the best in all Italy. He also said, 'I do beg of you to go to Italy; there one is esteemed and highly prized.' And in truth he is right. When I come to reflect on the subject, in no country have I received such honours, or been so esteemed as in Italy, and nothing contributes more to a man's fame than to have written Italian operas, and especially for Naples. He said he would write a letter for me to Santoro, which I was to copy out when I went to see him next day; but finding it impossible to return, he sent me a sketch of the letter today. I was told that when Misliweczeck heard people here speaking of Becke, or other performers on the piano, he invariably said, 'Let no one deceive himself; none can play like Mozart; in Italy, where the greatest masters are, they speak of no one but Mozart; when his name is mentioned not a word is said of others.' I can now write the letter to Naples when I please; but, indeed, the sooner the better. I should, however, first like to have the opinion of that highly discreet Hofcapellmeister, Herr von Mozart. I have the most ardent desire to write another opera. The distance is certainly great, but the period is still a long way off when I am to write this opera, and there may be many changes before then. I think I might at all events undertake it. If, in the meantime, I get no situation, *eh, bien!* I shall then have a resource in Italy. I am at all events certain to receive 100 ducats in the Carnival; and when I have once written for Naples I shall be sought for everywhere. As papa well knows, there is an opera buffa in Naples in spring, summer, and autumn, for which I might write for the sake of practice, not to be quite idle. It is true that there is not much to be got by this, but still there is something, and it would be the means of gaining more honour and reputation than by giving a hundred concerts in Germany, and I am far happier when I have something to compose, which is my chief delight and passion; and if I get a situation anywhere, or have hopes of one, the *scrittura* would be a great recommendation to me, and excite a sensation, and cause me to be more thought of. This is mere talk, but still I say what is in my heart. If papa gives me any good grounds to show that I am wrong, then I will give it up, though, I own, reluctantly. Even when I hear an opera discussed, or am in a theatre myself and hear voices, oh! I really am beside myself!

Tomorrow, mamma and I are to meet Misliweczeck in the Hospital garden to take leave of him; for he wished me last time to fetch mamma out of church, as he said he should like to see the mother of so great a virtuoso. My dear papa, do write to him as often as you have time to do so; you cannot confer a greater pleasure on him, for the man is quite forsaken. Sometimes he sees no one for a whole week, and he said to me, 'I do assure you it does seem so strange to me to see so few people; in Italy I had company every day.' He looks thin, of course, but is still full of fire and life and genius, and the same kind, animated person he always was. People talk much of his oratorio of 'Abraham and Isaac' which he produced here. He has just completed (with the exception of a few arias) a Cantata, or Serenata for Lent; and when he was at the worst he wrote an opera for Padua. Herr Heller is just come from him. When I wrote to him yesterday I sent him the Serenata that I wrote in Salzburg for the Archduke Maximilian ['Il Rè Pastore'].

Now to turn to something else. Yesterday I went with mamma immediately after dinner to take coffee with the two Fräulein von Freysinger. Mamma, however, took none, but drank two bottles of Tyrolese wine. At three o'clock she went home again to make preparations for our journey. I, however, went with the two ladies to Herr von Hamm's, whose three young ladies each played a concerto, and I one of Aichner's *prima vista*, and then went on extemporising. The teacher of these little simpletons, the Demoiselles Hamm, is a certain clerical gentleman of the name of Schreier. He is a good organ-player, but no pianist. He kept staring at me with an eyeglass. He is a reserved kind of man who does not talk much; he patted me on the shoulder, sighed, and said, 'Yes – you are – you understand – yes – it is true – you are an out-and-outer!' By the bye, can you recall the name of Freysingen – the papa of the two pretty girls I mentioned? He says he knows you well, and that he studied with you. He particularly remembers Messenbrunn, where papa (this was quite new to me) played most incomparably on the organ. He said, 'It was quite startling to see the pace at which both hands and feet went, but quite inimitable; a thorough master indeed; my father thought a great deal of him; and how he humbugged the priests about entering the church! You are just what he was then, as like as possible; only he was a degree shorter when I knew him.' *A propos*, a certain Hofrath Effeln sends you his kind regards; he is one of the best Hofraths here, and would long ago have been made chancellor but for one defect – *tippling*. When we saw him for the first time at Albert's, both mamma and I thought, 'What an odd-looking fish!' Just imagine a very tall man, stout and corpulent, and a ridiculous face. When he crosses the room to another table, he folds both hands on his stomach, stoops very low, and then draws himself up again, and makes little nods; and when this is over he draws back his right foot, and does this to each individual separately. He says that he knows papa intimately. I am now going for a little to the play. Next time I will write more fully, but I can't possibly go on today, for my fingers do ache uncommonly.

Munich, October 11th, at $\frac{1}{4}$ to 12 at night, I write as follows: – I have been at the Drittl comedy, but only went in time for the ballet, or rather the pantomime, which I had not before seen. It is called 'Das von der für *Girigaricanarimanarischaribari* verfertigte Ei.' It was very good and funny. We are going tomorrow to Augsburg on account of Prince Taxis not being at Ratisbon but at Teschingen. He is, in fact, at present at his country-seat, which is, however, only an hour from Teschingen. I send my sister, with this, four preludes; she will see and hear for herself the different keys into which they lead. My compliments to all my kind friends, particularly to young Count Arco, to Madlle. Sallerl, and to my best of all friends, Herr Bullinger; I do beg that next Sunday at the usual eleven o'clock music he will be so good as to make an authoritative oration in my name, and present my regards to all the members of the orchestra and exhort them to industry, that I may not one day be accused of being a humbug, for I have everywhere extolled their orchestra, and I intend always to do so.

Maria Anna Mozart continues

And I am sweating so that the water is pouring down my face, simply from the labour of packing. The devil take all travelling. I feel that I could shove my feet into my mug, I am so exhausted. I hope that you and Nannerl are well. I send most cordial greetings to my dear Sallerl and Monsieur Bullinger. Please tell Nannerl not to give Bimperl too much to eat, in case she should get too fat. I send greetings to Thresel. Addio. I kiss you both millions of times.

Maria Anna Mozart

Maria Anna Mozart to her Husband
Augsburg, 14 October 1777

We left Munich on the 11th at noon and arrived safely in Augsburg at nine in the evening; and this journey we did in nine hours with a hired coachman who, moreover, fed his horses for an hour.

Mozart continues
Augsburg, 14 October 1777

I have made no mistake in my date, for I write before dinner, and I think that next Friday, the day after tomorrow, we shall be off again. Pray hear how generous the gentlemen of Augsburg are. In no place was I ever so overwhelmed with marks of distinction as here. My first visit was to the Stadtpfleger Longo Tabarro [Burgomaster Langenmantl]. My cousin,* a good,

---

* Leopold Mozart had a brother in Augsburg, a bookbinder, whose daughter, 'das Bäsle' (the cousin), was two years younger than Mozart.

kind, honest man and worthy citizen, went with me, and had the honour to wait in the hall like a footman till my interview with the high and mighty Stadtpfleger was over. I did not fail first of all to present papa's respectful compliments. He deigned graciously to remember you, and said, 'And pray how have things gone with him?' 'Vastly well, God be praised!' I instantly rejoined, 'and I hope things have also gone well with you?' He then became more civil, and addressed me in the third person, so I called him 'Sir'; though, indeed, I had done so from the first. He gave me no peace till I went up with him to see his son-in-law (on the second floor), my cousin meanwhile having the pleasure of waiting in the staircase hall. I was obliged to control myself with all my might, or I must have given some polite hint about this. On going upstairs I had the satisfaction of playing for nearly three-quarters of an hour on a good clavichord of Stein's, in the presence of the stuck-up young son, and his prim condescending wife, and the simple old lady. I first extemporised, and then played all the music he had, *prima vista*, and among others some very pretty pieces of Edlmann's. Nothing could be more polite than they all were, and I was equally so, for my rule is to behave to people just as they behave to me; I find this to be the best plan. I said that I meant to go to Stein's after dinner, so the young man offered to take me there himself. I thanked him for his kindness, and promised to return at two o'clock. I did so, and we went

73

together in company with his brother-in-law, who looks a genuine student. Although I had begged that my name should not be mentioned, Herr von Langenmantl was so incautious as to say, with a simper, to Herr Stein, 'I have the honour to present to you a virtuoso on the piano.' I instantly protested against this, saying that I was only an indifferent pupil of Herr Sigl in Munich, who had charged me with a thousand compliments to him. Stein shook his head dubiously, and at length said, 'Surely I have the honour of seeing M. Mozart?' 'Oh, no,' said I; 'my name is Trazom, and I have a letter for you.' He took the letter and was about to break the seal instantly, but I gave him no time for that, saying, 'What is the use of reading the letter just now? Pray open the door of your saloon at once, for I am so very anxious to see your pianofortes.' 'With all my heart,' said he, 'just as you please; but for all that I believe I am not mistaken.' He opened the door, and I ran straight up to one of the three pianos that stood in the room. I began to play, and he scarcely gave himself time to glance at the letter, so anxious was he to ascertain the truth; so he only read the signature. 'Oh!' cried he, embracing me, and crossing himself and making all sorts of grimaces from intense delight. I will write to you another day about his pianos. He then took me to a coffee-house, but when we went in I really thought I must bolt, there was such a stench of tobacco-smoke, but for all that I was obliged to bear it for a good hour. I submitted to it all with a good grace, though I could have fancied that I was in Turkey. He made a great fuss to me about a certain Graf, a composer (of flute concertos only), and said, 'He is something quite extraordinary,' and every other possible exaggeration. I became first hot and then cold from nervousness. This Graf is a brother of the two who are in Harz and Zurich. He would not give up his intention, but took me straight to him – a dignified gentleman indeed; he wore a dressing gown that I would not be ashamed to wear in the street. All his words are on stilts, and he has a habit of opening his mouth before knowing what he is going to say; so he often shuts it again without having said anything. After a great deal of ceremony he produced a concerto for two flutes; I was to play first violin. The concerto is confused, not natural, too abrupt in its modulations, and devoid of all genius. When it was over I praised it highly, for, indeed, he deserves this. The poor man must have had labour and study enough to write it. At last they brought a clavichord of Stein's out of the next room, a very good one, but inch-thick with dust. Herr Graf, who is director here, stood there looking like a man who had hitherto believed his own modulations to be something very clever, but all at once discovers that others may be still more so, and without grating on the ear. In a word, they all seemed lost in astonishment.

Mozart to his Father

Augsburg, 17 October 1777

I must now tell you about the Stein pianos. Before seeing these, Späth's pianos were my favourites; but I must
own that I give the preference to those of Stein, for they
damp much better than those in Ratisbon. If I strike
hard, whether I let my fingers rest on the notes or lift
them, the tone dies away at the same instant that it is
heard. Strike the keys as I choose, the tone always
remains even, never either jarring or failing to sound.
It is true that a piano of this kind is not to be had for
less than three hundred florins, but the pains and skill
which Stein bestows on them cannot be sufficiently
repaid. His instruments have a feature of their own; they
are supplied with a peculiar escapement. Not one in a
hundred makers attends to this; but, without it, it is
impossible that a piano should not buzz and jar. His
hammers fall as soon as they touch the strings, whether
the keys be held down by the fingers or not. When he
has completed an instrument of this class (which he told
me himself), he tries all kinds of passages and runs on it,
and works away at it, testing its powers till it is capable
of doing anything, for he labours not for his own benefit
alone (or he might be saved much trouble), but for that
of music. He often says, 'If I were not such a passionate
lover of music, playing also myself a little on the piano,
I should long ago have lost patience with my work, but

I like my instruments to respond to the player, and to be durable.' His pianos do really last well. He warrants the sounding-board neither breaking nor cracking; when he has finished one, he exposes it in the air to rain, snow, sun, and every kind of devilry, that it may give way, and then inserts slips of wood which he glues in, making it quite strong and solid. He is very glad when it does crack, for then he is pretty sure nothing further can happen to it. He frequently makes cuts into them himself, and then glues them up, thus making them doubly strong. He has three of these pianos at this moment finished, and I played on them again today ...

Leopold Mozart to his Wife and Son
Salzburg, 23 October 1777

My Dear Wife!

Tell Wolfgang that the Court Baker's saucer-eyed daughter who danced with him at the Stern, who often paid him friendly compliments and who ended by entering the convent at Loreto, has returned to her father's house. She heard that Wolfgang was going to leave Salzburg and probably hoped to see him again and to prevent him from doing so. Will Wolfgang be so kind as to refund to her father the money which the pomp and all the fine preparation for entering her convent cost him! You are still in Augsburg? Bravissimo! ... Of course, if you want to give a concert, you must make it known several days in advance. I only hope that it may be profitable! Though I doubt whether it will bring in much. Everyone who comes will probably pay one gulden, twelve kreuzer; but will a great many turn up? *I am very curious to hear all about it . . .*

Mon très cher Fils!

I am to wish you happiness on your name-day! But what can I now wish you that I do not always wish you? And that is, the grace of God, that it may follow you everywhere, that it may never leave you. And this it will never do, if you are diligent in fulfilling the duties of a true Catholic Christian. You know me. I am no pedant and no praying Peter and still less am I a hypocrite. But surely you will not refuse the request of a father, that you should take thought for the welfare of your soul so that in the hour of his death you may cause him no anxiety, and that in that dread moment he may have no reason to reproach himself for not having watched over your soul's salvation. Farewell! Be happy! Be sensible! Honour and care for your mother, who is having much anxiety in her old age. Love me as I love you. Your truly affectionate father

Leop. Mozart

Maria Anna Mozart to her Husband
Augsburg, 23 October 1777

Today, the 23rd, Wolfgang is lunching again at the Holy Cross Monastery and I too was invited, but as the cold has given me pains in my belly, I have stayed at home. Is it as cold at Salzburg as it is here, where everything is frozen hard just as if it were midwinter? If nothing prevents us, we intend to leave for Wallerstein on the day after tomorrow Saturday. The concert here was a tremendous success. The papers will tell you more. Herr Stein took infinite trouble and gave us every assistance. You must write him a letter and thank him. I hope that you and Nannerl are in good health, but somehow I am dreadfully anxious in case you should be unwell, as we have not had a line from you this week. Do write to me soon and relieve me of my anxiety. I am very much surprised that you have not received the Schuster duets –

Mozart continues
Augsburg, 23 October 1777

Why, of course he has received them.
Mamma. Not at all, he has kept on writing that he has not yet received them.
Wolfgang. I detest arguing. He has certainly got them and that's an end of it.

79

Mamma. You are wrong, Wolfgang.

Wolfgang. No, I am right. I will show it to Mamma in black and white.

Mamma. Where then?

Wolfgang. There, read that.

Mamma is reading your letter now.

Last Sunday I attended service at the Holy Cross, and at ten o'clock we went to Herr Stein's, where we tried over a couple of symphonies for the concert. Afterwards I dined with my cousin at the Holy Cross, where a band played during dinner. Badly as they play in the monastery, I prefer it to the Augsburg orchestra. I played a symphony, and a concerto in B of Vanhall's, on the violin, with unanimous applause. The Dean is a kind, jovial man, a cousin of Eberlin [deceased Capellmeister of Salzburg]. His name is Zeschinger. He knows papa well. At night, after supper, I played the Strassburg concerto; it went as smooth as oil; every one praised the fine pure tone. A small clavichord was then brought in, on which I preluded, and played a sonata and the Fischer variations. Some of those present whispered to the Dean that he ought to hear me play in the organ style. I asked him to give me a theme, which he declined, but one of the monks did so. I handled it quite leisurely, and all at once (the fugue being in G minor) I brought in a lively movement in the major key, but in the same tempo, and then at the end the original subject, only reversed. At last it occurred to me to employ the lively movement for the subject of the fugue also. I did not hesitate long, but did so at once, and it went as accurately as if Daser [a Salzburg tailor] had taken its measure. The Dean was in a state of great excitement. 'It is over,' said he, 'and it's no use talking about it, but I could scarcely have believed what I have just heard; you are indeed an able man. My prelate told me beforehand that in his life he never heard any one play the organ in a more finished and solid style' (he having heard me some days previously when the Dean was not here). At last some one brought me a fugued sonata, and asked me to play it. But I said, 'Gentlemen, I really must say this is asking rather too much, for it is not likely I shall be able to play such a sonata at sight.' 'Indeed, I think so too; it is too much; no one could do it,' said the Dean eagerly, being all in my favour. 'At all events,' said I, 'I can but try.' I heard the Dean muttering all the time behind me, 'Oh, you rogue! oh, you knave!' I played till 11 o'clock, bombarded and besieged, as it were, by fugue themes.

Lately, at Stein's, he brought me a sonata of Becke's, but I think I already told you this. *A propos*, as to his little girl,* any one who can see and hear her play without laughing must be Stein [stone] like her father. She perches herself exactly opposite the treble, avoiding the centre, that she may have more room to throw herself

---

* Nanette, at that time eight years old; afterwards, the admirable wife of Andreas Streicher, the friend of Schiller's youth, and one of Beethoven's best friends in Vienna.

about and make grimaces. She rolls her eyes and smirks; when a passage comes twice she always plays it slower the second time, and if three times slower still. She raises her arms in playing a passage, and if it is to be played with emphasis she seems to give it with her elbows and not her fingers, as awkwardly and heavily as possible. The finest thing is, that if a passage occurs (which ought to flow like oil) where the fingers must necessarily be changed, she does not pay much heed to that, but lifts her hands, and quite coolly goes on again. This, moreover, puts her in a fair way to get hold of a wrong note, which often produces a curious effect. I only write this in order to give you some idea of pianoforte-playing and teaching here, so that you may in turn derive some benefit from it. Herr Stein is quite infatuated about his daughter. She is eight years old, and learns everything by heart. She may one day be clever, for she has genius, but on this system she will never improve, nor will she ever acquire much velocity of finger, for her present method is sure to make her hand heavy. She will never master what is the most difficult and necessary, and in fact the principal thing in music, namely, time; because from her infancy she has never been in the habit of playing in correct time. Herr Stein and I discussed this point together for at least two hours. I have, however, in some degree converted him; he asks my advice now on every subject. He was quite devoted to Becke, and now he sees and hears that I can do more than Becke, that I make no grimaces, and yet play with so much expression that he himself acknowledges none of his acquaintances have ever handled his pianos as I do. My keeping so accurately in time causes them all much surprise. The left hand being quite independent in the *tempo rubato* of an adagio, they cannot at all comprehend. With them the left hand always yields to the right. Count Wolfeck and others, who have a passionate admiration for Becke, said lately publicly in a concert that I beat Becke hollow. Count Wolfeck went round the room saying, 'In my life I never heard anything like this.' He said to me, 'I must tell you that I never heard you play as you did today, and I mean to say so to your father as soon as I go to Salzburg.' What do you think was the first piece after the symphony? The concerto for three pianos. Herr Demmler took the first part, I the second, and Herr Stein the third. I then played a solo, my last sonata in D, for Durnitz, and afterwards my concerto in B; then again a solo in the organ style, namely, a fugue in C minor, then all of a sudden a splendid sonata in C major, finishing with a rondo, all extempore. What a noise and commotion there was! Herr Stein did nothing but make faces and grimaces of astonishment. Herr Demmler was seized with fits of laughter, for he is a queer creature, and when anything pleases him exceedingly, he can't help laughing heartily; indeed, on this occasion he actually began to swear! *Addio!*

Mozart to his Father

Augsburg, 25 October 1777

The receipts of the concert were 90 florins, without
deducting the expenses. Including, therefore, the two
ducats we took in the Casino concert, we had 100 florins.
The expenses of the concert did not exceed 16 florins
30 kreuzers; the room I had gratis. I believe most of the
musicians will make no charge. We have now *altogether*
lost about 26 or 27 florins. This is not of much moment.
I am writing this on Saturday the 25th. This morning
early I received the letter with the sad news of Frau
Oberbereiterin's death. Madlle. Tonerl can now purse
up her mouth, or perhaps open it wide, and shut it again
as empty as ever. As to the baker's daughter, I have no
objection to make; I foresaw all this long ago. This was
the cause of my reluctance to leave home, and finding it
so difficult to go. I hope the affair is not by this time
known all over Salzburg? I beg you, dear papa, most
urgently to keep the matter quiet as long as possible, and
in the meantime to pay her father on my account any
expenses he may have incurred by her entrance into the
convent, which I will repay gladly when I return to
Salzburg.

I thank you most truly, dear papa, for your good
wishes on my name-day. Do not be uneasy on my
account, for I have always God before my eyes, I
acknowledge His omnipotence, I dread His wrath;
but I also know His love, His compassion and mercy

towards His creatures, and that He will never forsake His servants. When His will is done I am resigned; so I never can fail to be happy and contented. I shall certainly also strive to live as strictly as possible in accordance with your injunctions and advice. Thank Herr Bullinger a thousand times for his congratulations. I mean to write to him soon and thank him myself, but I may in the meantime assure him that I neither know nor have any better, more sincere, or truer friend than himself. I beg also humbly to thank Madlle. Sallerl; pray tell her I mean to enclose some verses to show my gratitude to her in my letter to Herr Bullinger. Thank my sister also; she is to keep the Schuster duetts, and give herself no further trouble on the subject.

In your first letter, dear papa, you write that I lowered myself by my conduct to that lad Langenmantl. Anything but that! I was only straightforward, no more. I see you think he is still a boy; he is one or two and twenty, and a married man. Can any one be considered a boy who is married? I have never gone near him since. I left two cards for him today, and excused myself for not going in, having so many indispensable calls to make. I must now conclude, for mamma insists *absolument* on going to dinner, and then to pack. Tomorrow we go straight to Wallerstein. My dear little cousin, who sends you her regards, is anything but a prude. She dressed *à la Française* to please me yesterday. She looked at least 5 per cent. prettier in consequence. Now, *Addio!*

Mozart to his Father

Mannheim, 4 November 1777

I am at Cannabich's every day, and mamma went with
me there today. He is a very different man from what he
formerly was,* and the whole orchestra say the same.
He is very fond of me. He has a daughter who plays the
piano very nicely, and in order to make him still more
friendly towards me I am working just now at a sonata
for her, which is finished all but the Rondo. When I had
completed the first *allegro* and *andante*, I took it to him
myself and played it over; you can't think what applause
this sonata receives. There chanced to be some of the
musicians there at the moment – young Danner, Lang,
who plays the French horn, and the hautboy-player,
whose name I forget, but who plays remarkably well,
and has a pleasing delicate tone [Ramm]. I made him a
present of a concerto for the hautboy; it is being copied
in Cannabich's room. The man is wild with delight.
I played him the concerto today at Cannabich's, and
though known to be mine it pleased very much. No one
said that it was *not well composed*, because people here
don't understand these things. They ought to apply to
the Archbishop; he would soon put them on the right
scent.** I played all my six sonatas today at

* Mozart had been at his house, when a boy, with his father.
** The Archbishop never was satisfied with any of the compositions
that Mozart wrote for his concerts, but invariably had some fault to
find with them.

Cannabich's. Herr Kapellmeister Holzbauer went with me today to Count Savioli's. Cannabich was there at the time. Herr Holzbauer said to the Count in Italian that I wished to have the honour of playing before his Serene Highness the Elector. 'I was here fifteen years ago,' said I, 'but now I am older and more advanced, and I may say in music also ———' 'Oh!' said the Count, 'you are ———' I have no idea whom he took me for, as Cannabich interrupted him, but I affected not to hear, and entered into conversation with the others. Still I observed that he was speaking of me very earnestly. The Count then said to me, 'I hear that you play the piano very tolerably?' I bowed...

Mozart to his Cousin, Maria Anna Thekla Mozart, Augsburg

Mannheim, 5 November 1777

My dear Coz – Buzz,

I have safely received your precious epistle – thistle, and from it I perceive – achieve, that my aunt – gaunt, and you – shoe, are quite well – bell. I have today a letter – setter, from my papa – ah-ha, safe in my hands – sands. I hope you also got – trot, my Mannheim letter – setter. Now for a little sense – pence. The prelate's seizure – leisure, grieves me much – touch, but he will, I hope, get well – sell. You write – blight, you will keep – cheap, your promise to write to me – he-he, to

87

Augsburg soon – spoon. Well, I shall be very glad – mad. You further write, indeed you declare, you pretend, you hint, you vow, you explain, you distinctly say, you long, you wish, you desire, you choose, command, and point out, you let me know and inform me that I must send you my portrait soon – moon. *Eh, bien!* you shall have it before long – song. Now I wish you good night – tight.

The 5th. – Yesterday I conversed with the illustrious Electress; and tomorrow, the 6th, I am to play in the gala concert, and afterwards, by desire of the Princess, in their private apartments. Now for something rational! I beg of you – why not? – I beg of you, my very dear cousin – why not? – when you write to Madame Tavernier in Munich, to convey a message from me to the two Demoiselles Freysinger – why not? odd enough! but why not? – and I humbly ask pardon of Madlle. Josepha – I mean the youngest, and pray why not? why should I not ask her pardon? strange! but I don't know why I should not, so I do ask her pardon very humbly – for not having yet sent the sonata I promised her, but I mean to do so as soon as possible. Why not? I don't know why not. I can now write no more – which makes my heart sore. To all my kind friends much love – dove. Addio! Your old young, till death – breath,

Wolfgang Amadé Rosencranz
Miennham, eht ht5 rebotoc, 7771

Mozart to his Father

Mannheim, 13 November 1777

... Now for some of our news here. I was desired to
go yesterday with Cannabich to the Intendant, Count
Savioli, to receive my present. It was just what I had
anticipated – a handsome gold watch. Ten Carolins
would have pleased me better just now, though the
watch and chain, with its appendages, are valued at
twenty Carolins. Money is what is most needed on a
journey; and, by your leave, I have now five watches.
Indeed, I have serious thoughts of having a second
watch-pocket made, and, when I visit a grandee, to wear
two watches (which is indeed the fashion here), that no
one may ever again think of giving me another. I see
from your letter that you have not yet read Vogler's
book.* I have just finished it, having borrowed it from
Cannabich. His history is very short. He came here in a
miserable condition, performed on the piano, and composed a ballet. This excited the Elector's compassion,
who sent him to Italy. When the Elector was in
Bologna, he questioned Father Valoti about Vogler. 'Oh!
your Highness, he is a great man,' &c., &c. He then asked
Father Martini the same question. 'Your Highness,
he has talent; and by degrees, when he is older and
more solid, he will no doubt improve, though he must

* 'Ton Wissenschaft und Ton Kunst.'

first change considerably.' When Vogler came back he entered the Church, was immediately appointed Court Chaplain, and composed a *Miserere* which all the world declares to be detestable, being full of false harmony. Hearing that it was not much commended, he went to the Elector and complained that the orchestra played badly on purpose to vex and annoy him; in short, he knew so well how to make his game (entering into so many petty intrigues with women) that he became Vice-Capellmeister. He is a fool, who fancies that no one can be better or more perfect than himself. The whole orchestra, from the first to the last, detest him. He has been the cause of much annoyance to Holzbauer. His book is more fit to teach arithmetic than composition. He says that he can make a composer in three weeks, and a singer in six months; but we have not yet seen any proof of this. He despises the greatest masters. To myself he spoke with contempt of Bach [Johann Christian, J. Sebastian's youngest son, called the London Bach], who wrote two operas here, the first of which pleased more than the second, Lucio Silla. As I had composed the same opera in Milan, I was anxious to see it, and hearing from Holzbauer that Vogler had it, I asked him to lend it to me. 'With all my heart,' said he; 'I will send it to you tomorrow without fail, but you won't find much talent in it.' Some days after, when he saw me, he said with a sneer, 'Well, did you discover anything very fine – did you learn anything from it? One air is rather good. What are the words?' asked he of some person standing near. 'What air do you mean?' 'Why, that odious air of Bach's, that vile – oh! yes, *pupille amate*. He must have written it after a carouse of punch.' I really thought I must have laid hold of his pigtail; I affected, however, not to hear him, said nothing, and went away. He has now served out his time with the Elector.

The sonata for Madlle. Rosa Cannabich is finished. Last Sunday I played the organ in the chapel for my amusement. I came in while the *Kyrie* was going on, played the last part, and when the priest intoned the *Gloria* I made a cadence, so different, however, from what is usually heard here, that every one looked round in surprise, and above all Holzbauer. He said to me, 'If I had known you were coming, I would have put out another mass for you.' 'Oh!' said I, 'to puzzle me, I suppose?' Old Toeschi and Wendling stood all the time close beside me. I gave them enough to laugh at. Every now and then came a *pizzicato*, when I rattled the keys well; I was in my best humour. Instead of the *Benedictus* here, there is always a voluntary, so I took the ideas of the *Sanctus* and worked them out in a fugue. There they all stood making faces. At the close, after *Ita missa est*, I played a fugue. Their pedal is different from ours, which at first rather puzzled me, but I soon got used to it. I must now conclude. Pray write to us still at Mannheim. I know all about Misliweczeck's sonatas, and played them lately at Munich; they are very easy and agreeable to listen to. My advice is that my sister, to whom I humbly commend myself, should play them with much expression, taste, and fire, and learn them by heart. For these are sonatas which cannot fail to please every one, are not difficult to commit to memory, and produce a good effect when played with precision.

Mozart to his Father
Mannheim, 14–16 November 1777

I, Johannes, Chrysostomus, Amadeus, Wolfgangus, Sigismundus, Mozart, plead guilty to having both yesterday and the day before (and very often besides) stayed away from home till twelve o'clock at night, from ten o'clock till the aforesaid hour, I being in the presence and company of M. Cannabich, his wife and daughter, the Herrn Schatzmeister, Ramm, and Lang, making doggerel rhymes with the utmost facility, in thought and word, but not in deed. I should not, however, have conducted myself in so reckless a manner if our ringleader, namely, the so-called Lisel (Elisabeth Cannabich), had not inveigled and instigated me to mischief, and I am bound to admit that I took great pleasure in it myself. I confess all these my sins and shortcomings from the depths of my heart, and in the hope of often having similar ones to confess, I firmly resolve to amend my present sinful life. I therefore beg for a dispensation if it can be granted; but, if not, it is a matter of indifference to me, for the game will go on all the same. *Lusus enim suum habet ambitum*, says the pious singer Messner (chap. 9, p. 24), and also the pious Ascenditor, patron of singed coffee, musty lemonade, milk of almonds with no almonds in it, and, above all, strawberry ice full of lumps of ice, being himself a great connoisseur and artist in these delicacies.

The sonata I composed for Madlle. Cannabich I intend to write out as soon as possible on small paper, and to send it to my sister. I began to teach it to Madlle. Rose three days ago, and she has learned the *allegro*. The *andante* will give us most trouble, for it is full of expression, and must be played with accuracy and taste, and the *fortes* and *pianos* given just as they are marked. She is very clever, and learns with facility. Her right hand is very good, but the left is unhappily quite ruined. I must say that I do really feel very sorry for her, when I see her labouring away till she is actually panting for breath; and this not from natural awkwardness on her part, but because, being so accustomed to this method, she cannot play in any other way, never having been shown the right one. I said, both to her mother and herself, that if I were her regular master I would lock up all her music, cover the keys of the piano with a handkerchief, and make her exercise her right and left hand, at first quite slowly in nothing but passages and shakes, &c., until her hands were thoroughly trained; and after that I should feel confident of making her a genuine pianiste. They both acknowledged that I was right. It is a sad pity; for she has so much genius, reads very tolerably, has great natural aptitude, and plays with great feeling...

Mozart to his Father
Mannheim, 3 December 1777

I can still write nothing certain about my fate here. Last Monday, after going three days in succession to my *arch* pupils, morning and afternoon, I had the good fortune at last to meet the Elector. We all, indeed, thought that I had again come in vain, as it was so late in the day, but at length we saw him coming. The governess made the Countess seat herself at the piano, and I placed myself beside her to give her a lesson, and it was thus the Elector found us on entering. We rose, but he desired us to continue the lesson. When she had finished playing, the governess addressed him, saying that I had written a beautiful Rondo. I played it, and it pleased him exceedingly. At last he said, 'Do you think that she will be able to learn it?' 'Oh! yes,' said I; 'I only wish I had the good fortune to teach it to her myself.' He smiled, and said, 'I should also like it; but would it not be prejudicial to her to have two masters?' 'Oh! no, your Highness,' said I; 'it all depends on whether she has a good or a bad one. I hope your Highness will place trust and confidence in me.' 'Oh! assuredly,' said he. The governess then said, 'M. Mozart has also written these variations on the Fischer minuet for the young Count.' I played them, and he seemed to like them much. He now began to jest with the Countess. I thanked him for his present of a watch; he said, 'I must reflect on your wish; how long do you intend to remain here?' My answer was, 'As long as your Highness commands me to do so'; and then the interview was at an end. I went there again this morning, and was told that the Elector had repeated yesterday, 'Mozart stays here this winter.' Now I am fairly in for it; so you see I must wait...

Maria Anna Mozart adds a postscript
Mannheim, 3 December 1777

My dear Husband,

You see that I can't write very much to you, as Wolfgang has left me no room. In any case he has told you all there is to tell, so that I have no more news for you about our affairs. Often I just wish that I could spend at least one day with you, so that I could talk to you about all the things we cannot write about. To do so is quite impossible, for the letters would be far too long. We write to you twice every week, so you ought to get as many letters as we do. Addio. Keep well. I kiss you both many 100000 times and remain your faithful wife

Maria Anna Mozart

All sorts of messages to all our acquaintances.

Maria Anna Mozart to her Husband
Mannheim, 11 December 1777

My dear Husband,

You insist on knowing how much we have spent on our journey. We told you about Albert's account and that our bill in Augsburg was 300 gulden. Wolfgang told you that we were 24 gulden on the wrong side; but he forgot to include the expenses of the concert, which were 16 gulden, and also our landlord's account. Thus by the time we got to Mannheim we had only about 60 gulden in total. So if we had gone off again after a fortnight, we should not have had much left. For travelling expenses have gone up a lot since everything has become so dear. It is not anything like what it used to be, you would be surprised. As for Wolfgang's journey to Paris, you must think it over and let us know if you approve. At this time of the year Paris is the only place where there is anything doing. Monsieur Wendling is an honest fellow, as everybody knows. He has travelled far and wide and has been to Paris thirteen times already. He knows every stick and stone there; and our friend Herr Grimm is his best friend and has done a lot for him. So make up your mind, whatever you decide will suit me. Herr Wendling has assured me that he will be a father to Wolfgang, whom he loves as if he were his own son; and Wolfgang will be looked after as well as if he were with me. As you may imagine, I do not like to let him go, nor do I like to have to travel home alone, it is such an awful distance. I can't bear to think of it. But what can we do? I am too old to undertake such a long journey to Paris and besides it would cost too much. To travel à quatre is much cheaper than to find all one's expenses oneself. I shall write more next post-day. Today I have a headache and I think I am due for a cold. It is bitterly cold here. I am so frozen that I can hardly hold my pen. Wolfgang has gone out to look at lodgings. The cheap ones are very scarce here, but there are plenty of expensive ones. Tell Nannerl that people do not wear jackets here except indoors. Out-of-doors they wear chiefly cloaks and capes. The caps they wear are much prettier than what we wear in Salzburg and quite different – their frisure is quite wonderful, nothing piled up at all. The women are dressed very smartly. If it were not such a distance, I would send Nannerl a cap and a Palatine. Addio. Keep well, both of you. I kiss you many 1000000 times and remain your faithful wife

Maria Anna Mozart

Mozart to his Father
Mannheim, 17 January 1778

Next Wednesday I am going for some days to Kirch-heim-Boland, the residence of the Princess of Orange. I have heard so much praise of her here that at last I have resolved to go. A Dutch officer, a particular friend of mine [M. de la Pottrie], was much upbraided by her, for not bringing me with him when he went to offer his new-year's congratulations. I expect to receive at least eight louis d'or, for as she has a passionate admiration of singing, I have had four arias copied out for her. I will also present her with a symphony, for she has a very nice orchestra and gives a concert every day. Besides, the copying of the airs will not cost me much, for a M. Weber who is going there with me has copied them. He has a daughter who sings admirably, and has a lovely pure voice; she is only fifteen.* She fails in nothing but in stage action; were it not for that, she might be the *prima donna* of any theatre. Her father is a downright honest German who brings up his children well, for which very reason the girl is persecuted here. He has six children – five girls and a son. He and his wife and children have been obliged to live for the last fourteen years on an income of 200 florins, but as he has always done his duty well, and has lately provided a very accomplished singer for the Elector, he has now actually 400 florins. My aria for De' Amicis she sings to perfection with all its tremendous passages: she is to sing it at Kirchheim-Boland.

Now for another subject. Last Wednesday there was a great feast in our house [at Hofkammerrath Serrarius's] to which I was also invited. There were

---

* Aloysia, second daughter of the prompter and theatrical copyist, Weber, a brother of Carl Maria von Weber's father.

fifteen guests, and the young lady of the house [Pierron, the 'House Nymph'] was to play in the evening the concerto I had taught her at eleven o'clock in the forenoon. The Herr Kammerrath and Herr Vogler called on me. Herr Vogler seems quite determined to become acquainted with me, as he often importuned me to go to see him, but he has overcome his pride and paid me the first visit. Besides, people tell me that he is now very different, being no longer so much admired; for at first he was made quite an idol of here. We went upstairs together, when by degrees the guests assembled, and there was no end to talking. After dinner Vogler sent for two pianos of his, which were tuned alike, and also his wearisome engraved sonatas. I had to play them, while he accompanied me on the other piano. At his urgent request I sent for my sonatas also. N.B. – Before dinner he had scrambled through my sonata at sight (the Litzau one which the young lady of the house plays). He took the first part *prestissimo* – the *Andante allegro* – and the Rondo more *prestissimo* still. He played great part of the bass very differently from the way in which it is written, inventing at times quite another harmony and melody. It is impossible to do otherwise in playing at such a pace, for the eyes cannot see the notes, nor the hands get hold of them. What merit is there in this? The listeners (I mean those worthy of the name) can only say that they have *seen* music and piano-playing. All this makes them hear, and think, and feel as little – as he does. You may easily believe that this was beyond all endurance, because I could not venture to say to him *much too quick!* besides, it is far easier to play a thing quickly than slowly; some notes may then be dropped without being observed. But is this genuine music? In rapid playing the right and left hands may be changed, and no one either see or hear it; but is this good? and in what does the art of reading *prima vista* consist? In this – to play the piece in the time in which it ought to be played, and to express all the notes and apoggiaturas, &c., with proper taste and feeling as written, so that it should give the impression of being composed by the person who plays it. His fingering also is miserable; his left thumb is just like that of the late Adlgasser, and all the runs downwards with the right hand, he makes with his first finger and thumb!

Mozart to his Father
Mannheim, 4 February 1778

I could not delay writing to you till the usual Saturday arrived, because it was so long since I had the pleasure of conversing with you by means of my pen. The first thing I mean to write about is how my worthy friends and I got on at Kirchheim-Boland. It was simply a holiday excursion, and nothing more. On Friday morning at eight o'clock we drove away from here, after I had breakfasted with Herr Weber. We had a capital covered coach which held four; at four o'clock we arrived at Kirchheim-Boland. We immediately sent a list of our names to the palace. Next morning early, Herr Concertmeister Rothfischer called on us. He had been already described to me at Mannheim as a most honourable man, and such I find him to be. In the evening we went to court (this was on Saturday), where Madlle. Weber sang three airs. I say nothing of her singing, but it is indeed admirable. I wrote to you lately with regard to her merits; but I cannot finish this letter without writing further about her, as I have only recently known her well, so now first discover her great powers. We dined afterwards at the officers' table. Next day we went some distance to church, for the Catholic one is rather far away. This was on Sunday. In the forenoon we dined again with the officers. In the evening there was no music, because it was Sunday. Thus they have music only 300 times during the year. In the evening we might have supped at court, but we preferred being all together at the inn. We would gladly have made them a present also of the dinners at the officers' table, for we were never so pleased as when by ourselves; but economy rather entered our thoughts, since we were obliged to pay heavily enough at the inn.

The following day, Monday, we had music again, and also on Tuesday and Wednesday. Madlle. Weber sang in all thirteen times, and played twice on the piano, for she plays by no means badly. What surprises me most is that she reads music so well. Only think of her playing my difficult sonatas at sight, *slowly*, but without missing a single note. I give you my honour I would rather hear my sonatas played by her than by Vogler. I played twelve times, and once by desire, on the organ of the Lutheran church. I presented the Princess with four symphonies, and received only seven louis d'or in silver, and our poor dear Madlle. Weber only five. This I certainly did not anticipate! I never expected great things, but at all events I hoped that each of us would at least receive eight louis d'or. *Basta!* We were not, however, losers, for I have a profit of forty-two florins, and the inexpressible pleasure of becoming better acquainted with worthy upright Christian people, and good Catholics. I regret much not having known them long ago.

The 4th. – Now comes something urgent, about which I request an answer. Mamma and I have discussed the matter, and we agree that we do not like the sort of life the Wendlings lead. Wendling is a very honourable and kind man, but unhappily devoid of all religion, and the whole family are the same. I say enough when I tell you that his daughter was a most disreputable character. Ramm is a good fellow, but a libertine. I know myself, and I have such a sense of religion that I shall never do anything which I would not do before the whole world; but I am alarmed even at the very thoughts of being in the society of people, during my journey, whose mode of thinking is so entirely different from mine (and from that of all good people). But of course they must do as they please. I have no heart to travel with them, nor could I enjoy one pleasant hour, nor know what to talk about; for, in short, I have no great confidence in them. Friends who have no religion cannot be long our friends. I have already given them a hint of this by saying that during my absence three letters had arrived, of which I could for the present divulge nothing further than that it was unlikely I should be able to go with them to Paris, but that perhaps I might come later, or possibly go elsewhere; so they must not depend on me. I shall be able to finish my music now quite at my ease for De Jean, who is to give me 200 florins for it. I can remain here as long as I please, and neither board nor lodging cost me anything. In the meantime Herr Weber will endeavour to make various engagements for concerts with me, and then we shall travel together. If I am with him, it is just as if I were with you. This is the reason that I like him so much – except in personal appearance, he resembles you in all respects, and has exactly your character and mode of thinking. If my mother were not, as you know, too *comfortably lazy* to write, she would say precisely what I do. I must confess that I much enjoyed my excursion with them. We were pleased and merry; I heard a man converse just like you; I had no occasion to trouble myself about anything; what was torn I found repaired. In short, I was treated like a prince. I am so attached to this oppressed family that my greatest wish is to make them happy, and perhaps I may be able to do so. My advice is that they should go to Italy, so I am all anxiety for you to write to our good friend Lugiati [impresario], and the sooner the better, to enquire what are the highest terms given to a *prima donna* in Verona – the more the better, for it is always easy to accept lower terms. Perhaps it would be possible to obtain the *Ascensa* in Venice. I will be answerable with my life for her singing, and her doing credit to my recommendation. She has, even during this short period, derived much profit from me, and how much further progress she will have made by that time! I have no fears either with regard to her acting. If this plan be realised, M. Weber, his two daughters, and I, will have the happiness of visiting my dear papa and dear sister for a fortnight, on our way through Salzburg. My sister will find a friend and companion in Madlle. Weber, for, like my sister in Salzburg, she enjoys the best reputation here, owing to the careful way in which she has been brought up; the father resembles you, and the whole family that of Mozart. They have indeed detractors, as with us, but when it comes to the point they must confess the truth; and truth lasts longest. I should be so glad to go with them to Salzburg, that you might hear her. My air that De' Amicis used to sing, and the bravura aria *'Parto m' affretto'*, and *'Dalla sponda tenebrosa'*, she sings splendidly. Pray do all you can to insure our going to Italy together. You know my greatest desire is — to write operas.

I will gladly write an opera for Verona for thirty zecchini, solely that Madlle. Weber may acquire fame by it; for, if I do not, I fear she may be sacrificed. Before then I hope to make so much money by visiting different places that I shall be no loser. I think we shall go to Switzerland, perhaps also to Holland; pray write to me soon about this. Should we stay long anywhere, the eldest daughter [Josepha, afterwards Madame Hofer, for whom the part of the Queen of the Night in the 'Flauto magico' was written] would be of the greatest use to us; for we could have our own *ménage*, as she understands cooking.

Send me an answer soon, I beg. Don't forget my wish to write an opera; I envy every person who writes one; I could almost weep from vexation when I hear or see an aria. But Italian, not German – *seria*, not *buffa*! I have now written you all that is in my heart; my mother is satisfied with my plan.

Maria Anna Mozart to her Husband
Mannheim, 5 February 1778

No doubt you perceive by the accompanying letter that when Wolfgang makes new friends he would give his life for them. It is true that she does sing incomparably; still, we ought not to lose sight of our own interests.

I never liked his being in the society of Wendling and Ramm, but I did not venture to object to it, nor would he have listened to me; but no sooner did he know these Webers than he instantly changed his mind. In short, he prefers other people to me, for I remonstrate with him sometimes, and that he does not like. I write this quite secretly while he is at dinner, for I don't wish him to know it.

Mozart to his Father
Mannheim, 7 February 1778

... In my last letter I forgot to mention Mlle Weber's greatest merit, which is her superb cantabile singing. Please do not forget about Italy. I commend this poor, but excellent little Mlle Weber to your interest with all my heart, *caldamente*, as the Italians say. I have given her three of De Amicis's arias, the scena I wrote for Madame Duschek (to whom I shall be writing soon) and four arias from 'Il Rè pastore'. I have also promised her to have some arias sent from home. I hope you will be kind enough to send them to me, but send them *gratis*, I beg you, and you will really be doing a good turn! You will find the list of them on the French song which her father has copied out, and the paper is part of a present from him; but indeed he has given me much more. Now I must close ...

Leopold Mozart to his Son
Salzburg, 11–12 February 1778

My dear Son!

I have read your letter of the 4th with astonishment
and horror. I am beginning to answer it today, the 11th,
for the whole night long I was unable to sleep and am
so exhausted that I can only write quite slowly, word
by word, and so gradually finish what I have to say by
tomorrow. Up to the present, thank God, I have been
in good health; but this letter, in which I only recognize
my son by that failing of his which makes him believe
everyone at the first word spoken, open his kind heart
to every persuasive flatterer and let others sway him as
they like, so that he is led by fantastic ideas and ill-
considered and unpractical projects to sacrifice his own
name and interests, and even the interests and the
claims of his aged and honourable parents to those of
strangers – this letter, I say, depressed me exceedingly,
the more so as I was cherishing the reasonable hope
that certain circumstances which you had had to face
already, as well as my own reminders, both spoken and
written, could not have failed to convince you that not
only for the sake of your happiness but in order that you
may be able to earn a living and attain at length the
desired goal in a world of men in varying degrees good
and bad, fortunate and unfortunate, it was imperative
for you to guard your warm heart by the strictest

reserve, undertake nothing without full consideration and never let yourself be carried away by enthusiastic impulses and blind fancies. My dear son, I implore you to read this letter carefully – and take time to reflect upon it. Merciful God! those happy days are gone when, as child and boy, you never went to bed without standing on a chair and singing to me *Oragna fiagata fà*, and ending by kissing me again and again on the tip of my nose and telling me that when I grew old you would put me in a glass case and protect me from every breath of air, so that you might always have me with you and honour me. Listen to me, therefore, in patience! You are fully acquainted with our difficulties in Salzburg – you know my wretched income, why I kept my promise to let you go away, and all my various troubles. The purpose of your journey was twofold – either to get a good permanent appointment, or, if this should fail, to go off to some big city where large sums of money can be earned. Both plans were designed to assist your parents and your dear sister, but above all to build up your own reputation in the world ...

... You took that journey to Munich – with what purpose you know – but nothing could be done. Well-meaning friends wanted to keep you there and you wished to remain ...

... At that time you were quite amazingly taken up with the little singer at the theatre and your dearest wish was to forward the cause of the German stage; now you declare that you would not even care to write a comic opera! No sooner had you left the gates of Munich behind you than (as I prophesied) your whole company of subscribers had forgotten you. What would be your fate if you were in Munich now? – In the end one can always see the hand of God. In Augsburg too you had your little romance, you amused yourself with my brother's daughter, who now must needs send you her portrait ... When you were in Mannheim you did well to win the good graces of Herr *Cannabich*. But you would have gained nothing, had he not been seeking a double advantage therefrom. I have already written to you about the rest. Next, Herr Cannabich's daughter was praised to the sky, her character celebrated in the Adagio of a sonata, in short, *she* was now the reigning favourite. Then you made the acquaintance of Herr Wendling. *He* was now the most honourable friend – and what happened next, I need not repeat. Suddenly you strike up a new acquaintanceship – with Herr Weber; all your other friends are forgotten; now *this family* is the most honourable, the most Christian family and the daughter is to have the leading role in the tragedy to be enacted between your own family and hers! In the transports into which your kind and too generous heart has thrown you, you think all your extravagant fancies as reasonable and practicable as if they were bound to be accomplished in the normal course of nature. You are thinking of taking her to Italy

109

as a prima donna. Tell me, do you know of any prima donna who, without having first appeared many times in Germany, has walked on to the stage in Italy as prima donna? ... What impresario would not laugh, were one to recommend him a girl of sixteen or seventeen, who has never yet appeared on a stage! As for your proposal (I can hardly write when I think of it), your proposal to travel about with Herr Weber and, be it noted, his two daughters – it has nearly made me lose my reason! My dearest son! How can you have allowed yourself to be bewitched even for an hour by such a horrible idea, which must have been suggested to you by someone or other! Your letter reads like a romance. For could you really make up your mind to go trailing about the world with strangers? Quite apart from your reputation – what of your old parents and your dear sister? To expose me to the mockery and ridicule of the Prince and of *the whole town which loves you?* Yes, to expose me to mockery and yourself to contempt, for in reply to repeated questions, I have had to tell everyone that you were going to Paris. And now, after all, you want to roam about with strangers and take your chance? Surely, after a little reflection you will give up all idea of doing so! But that I may convince you of your folly, let me tell you that the time is now coming when no man in his senses could think of such a thing. Conditions are now such that it is impossible to guess where war may break out, for everywhere regiments are either on

110

the march or under marching orders. – To Switzerland? – To Holland? Why, there is not a soul there the whole summer; and at Berne and Zürich in winter one can just make enough not to die of starvation, but nothing more. As for Holland they have things to think of there besides music; and in any case half one's takings are eaten up by Herr Hummel and concert expenses. Besides, what will become of your reputation? Those are places for lesser lights, for second-rate composers, for scribblers, for a Schwindel, a Zappa, a Ricci and the like. Name any one great composer to me who would deign to take such an abject step! *Off with you to Paris!* and that soon! Find your place among great people. *Aut Caesar aut nihil.* The mere thought of seeing Paris ought to have preserved you from all these flighty ideas. *From Paris the name and fame of a man of great talent resounds throughout the whole world. There the nobility treat men of genius with the greatest deference, esteem and courtesy; there you will see a refined manner of life, which forms an astonishing contrast to the coarseness of our German courtiers and their ladies; and there you may become proficient in the French tongue* ... Your desire to help the oppressed you have inherited from your father. But you really must consider first of all the welfare of your parents, or else your soul will go to the devil. Think of me as you saw me when you left us, *standing beside the carriage in a state of utter wretchedness.* Ill as I was, I had been packing for you until two o'clock in the morning, and there I was at the carriage again at six o'clock, seeing to everything for you. Hurt me now, if you can be so cruel! Win fame and *make money* in Paris; then, *when you have money to spend*, go off to Italy and get commissions for operas. This cannot be done by writing letters to impresarios, though I am prepared to do so. Then you could put forward Mlle Weber's name, which can be the more easily done if you do so personally. Write to me by the next post without fail. We kiss you both a million times and I remain your old honest husband and father

MZT

Bullinger sends his greetings.

Nannerl has wept her full share during these last two days. Addio.

Mozart to his Father
Mannheim, 19 February 1778

I always thought that you would disapprove of my journey with the Webers, but I never had any such intention – I mean, *under present circumstances.* I gave them my word of honour to write to you to that effect. Herr Weber does not know how we stand, and I certainly shall tell it to no one. I wish my position had been such that I had no cause to consider any one else, and that we were all independent; but in the intoxication of the moment I forgot the present impossibility of the affair, and also to tell you what I had done. The reasons of my not being now in Paris must be evident to you from my last two letters. If my mother had not first begun on the subject, I certainly would have gone with my friends; but when I saw that she did not like it, I began to dislike it also. When people lose confidence in me, I am apt to lose confidence in myself. The days when, standing on a stool, I sang *Oragna fiagata fà*,* and at the end kissed the tip of your nose, are indeed gone by; but still, have my reverence, love, and obedience towards yourself ever failed on that account? I say no more. As for your reproach about the little singer in Munich, I must confess that I was an ass to write such a complete falsehood. She does not as yet know even what singing means. It was true that, for a person who had only learned music for three months, she sang surprisingly; and, besides, she has a pleasing pure voice. The reason why I praised her so much was probably my hearing people say, from morning to night, 'There is no better singer in all Europe; those who have not heard her have heard nothing.' I did not venture to disagree with them, partly because I wished to acquire friends, and partly because I had come direct from Salzburg, where we are not in the habit of contradicting any one; but as soon as I was alone I never could help laughing. Why, then, did I not laugh at her in my letter to you? I really cannot tell.

---

* Words sounding like Italian, but devoid of meaning, for which he had invented a melody. Nissen gives it in his Life of Mozart, p. 35.

The bitter way in which you write about my merry and innocent intercourse with your brother's daughter, makes me justly indignant; but as it is not as you think, I require to give you no answer on the subject. I don't know what to say about Wallerstein; I was very grave and reserved with Becke, and at the officers' table also I had a very serious demeanour, not saying one word to anybody. But let this all pass; you only wrote it in a moment of irritation. Your remarks about Madlle. Weber are just; but at the time I wrote to you I knew quite as well as you that she is still too young, and must be first taught how to act, and must rehearse frequently on the stage. But with some people one must proceed step by step. These good people are as tired of being here as —— you know *who* and *where* [meaning the Mozarts, father and son, in Salzburg], and they think everything feasible. I promised them to write everything to my father, but when the letter was sent off to Salzburg, I constantly told her that she must have a little patience, for she was still rather too young, &c. They take all I say in good part, for they have a high opinion of me. By my advice, Herr Weber has engaged Madlle. Toscani (an actress) to give his daughter lessons in acting. All you write of Madlle. Weber is true, except that she sings like a Gabrielli, for I should not at all like her to sing in that style. Those who have heard Gabrielli say, and must say, that she was only an adept in runs and *roulades*; but as she adopted so uncommon a reading she gained admiration, which, however, did not last longer than hearing her four times. She could not please in the long run, for roulades soon become very tiresome, and she had the misfortune of not being able to sing. She was not capable of sustaining a *breve* properly, and having no *messa di voce* she could not dwell on her notes; in short, she sang with skill, but devoid of intelligence. Madlle. Weber's singing, on the contrary, goes to the heart, and she prefers a *cantabile*. I have lately made her practise the passages in the Grand Aria, because, if she goes to Italy, it is necessary that she should sing bravuras. The *cantabile* she certainly will never forget, being her natural bent. Raaff (who is no flatterer), when asked to give his sincere opinion, said, 'She does not sing like a scholar, but like a professor.'

So now you know everything. I do still recommend her to you with my whole heart, and I beg you will not forget about the *arias, cadenzas,* &c. I can scarcely write from actual hunger. My mother will display the contents of our large moneybox. I embrace my sister lovingly. She is not to lament about every trifle, or I will never come back to her . . .

Mozart to his Cousin, Maria Anna Thekla Mozart, Augsburg
Mannheim, 28 February 1778

Mademoiselle, ma très-chère Cousine,

You perhaps think or believe that I must be dead? Not at all! I beg you will not think so, for how could I write so beautifully if I were dead? Could such a thing be possible? I do not attempt to make any excuses for my long silence, for you would not believe me if I did. But truth is truth; I have had so much to do that though I have had time to think of my cousin, I have had no time to write to her, so I was obliged to let it alone. But at last I have the honour to enquire how you are, and how you fare? If we soon shall have a talk? If you write with a lump of chalk? If I am sometimes in your mind? If to hang yourself you're inclined? If you're angry with me, poor fool? If your wrath begins to cool? – Oh! you are laughing! *Victoria!* I knew you could not long resist me, and in your favour would enlist me. Yes! yes! I know well how this is, though I'm in ten days off to Paris. If you write to me from pity, do so soon from Augsburg city, so that I may get your letter, which to me would be far better.

Now let us talk of other things. Were you very merry during the Carnival? They are much gayer at Augsburg at that time than here. I only wish I had been there that I might have frolicked about with you. Mamma and

I send our love to your father and mother, and to our cousin, and hope they are well and happy; better so, so better! *A propos*, how goes on your French? May I soon write you a French letter? from Paris, I suppose?

Now, before I conclude, which I must soon do because I am in haste (having just at this moment nothing to do), and also have no more room, as you see my paper is done, and I am very tired, and my fingers tingling from writing so much, and lastly even if I had room I don't know what I could say, except, indeed, a story which I have a great mind to tell you. So listen! It is not long since it happened, and in this very country too, where it made a great sensation, for really it seemed almost incredible, and, indeed, between ourselves, no one yet knows the result of the affair. So, to be brief, about four miles from here – I can't remember the name of the place, but it was either a village or a hamlet, or something of that kind. Well, after all, it don't much signify whether it was called Triebetrill or Burmsquick; there is no doubt that it was some place or other. There a shepherd or herdsman lived, who was pretty well advanced in years, but still looked strong and robust; he was unmarried and well-to-do, and lived happily. But before telling you the story, I must not forget to say that this man had a most astounding voice when he spoke; he terrified people when he spoke! Well! to make my tale as short as possible, you must know that he had a dog called Bellot, a very handsome large dog, white with black spots. Well! this shepherd was going along with his sheep, for he had a flock of eleven thousand under his care, and he had a staff in his hand, with a pretty rose-coloured topknot of ribands, for he never went out without his staff; such was his invariable custom. Now to proceed; being tired, after having gone a couple of miles, he sat down on a bank beside a river to rest. At last he fell asleep, when he dreamt that he had lost all his sheep, and this fear woke him, but to his great joy he saw his flock close beside him. At length he got up again and went on, but not for long; indeed, half an hour could scarcely have elapsed, when he came to a bridge which was very long, but with a parapet on both sides to prevent any one falling into the river. Well! he looked at his flock, and as he was obliged to cross the bridge, he began to drive over his eleven thousand sheep. Now be so obliging as to wait till the eleven thousand sheep are all safely across, and then I will finish the story. I already told you that the result is not yet known; I hope, however, that by the time I next write to you all the sheep will have crossed the bridge; but if not, why should I care? So far as I am concerned, they might all have stayed on this side. In the meantime you must accept the story so far as it goes; what I really know to be true I have written, and it is better to stop now than to tell you what is false, for in that case you would probably have discredited the whole, whereas now you will only disbelieve one half.

I must conclude, but don't think me rude; he who begins must cease, or the world would have no peace. My compliments to every friend, welcome to kiss me without end, for ever and a day, till good sense comes my way; and a fine kissing that will be, which frightens you as well as me. Adieu, ma chère cousine! I am, I was, I have been, oh! that I were, would to heavens I were! I will or shall be, would, could, or should be – what? – A blockhead!

W. A. M.

Mozart to his Father
Paris, 24 March 1778

Yesterday (Monday, the 23rd), at four o'clock in the afternoon, we arrived here, thank God! safely, having been nine days and a half on our journey. We thought we really could not have gone through with it; in my life I never was so wearied. You may easily imagine what it was to leave Mannheim and so many dear kind friends, and then to travel for ten days, not only without these friends, but without any human being – without a single soul whom we could associate with or even speak to. Now, thank Heaven! we are at our destination, and I trust that, with the help of God, all will go well ...

*The Paris visit was not a happy one for Mozart. He missed
the many friends he had left behind in Mannheim, he didn't
like the Parisians, and in spite of a promising start no commissions were forthcoming. His one achievement was the
'Paris' Symphony. And then, after only a few months in this
unfamiliar city, Mozart's mother suddenly became ill and
died on the night of 3 July. Few things in this correspondence
are more touching than the innocent deception Wolfgang
practised on his father in order to soften the unexpected blow,
writing a letter within a couple of hours of her death pretend-
ing that she was still only seriously ill, and immediately after
it, in the small hours of 4 July, another to a close friend in
Salzburg telling him the truth and begging him to go in
person to prepare his father for the news.*

Mozart to his Father
Paris, 14 May 1778

I have already so much to do that I don't know how
I am to manage when winter comes. I think I wrote to
you in my last letter that the Duc de Guines, whose
daughter is my pupil in composition, plays the flute
inimitably, and she the harp magnificently; she has a
great deal of talent and genius, and, above all, a wonderful memory, for she plays all her pieces, about 200 in
number, by heart. She, however, doubts much whether
she has any genius for composition, especially as
regards ideas or invention; but her father (who, *entre*

nous, is rather too infatuated about her) declares that she certainly has ideas, and that she is only too diffident and has too little self-reliance. Well, we shall see. If she acquires no thoughts or ideas (for hitherto she really has none whatever), it is all in vain, for God knows I can't give her any! It is not the father's intention to make her a great composer. He says, 'I don't wish her to write operas, or arias, or concertos, or symphonies, but grand sonatas for her instrument and for mine.' I gave her today her fourth lesson on the rules of composition and harmony, and am pretty well satisfied with her. She made a very good bass for the first minuet, of which I had given her the melody, and she has already begun to write in three parts; she can do it, but she quickly tires, and I cannot get her on, for it is impossible to proceed further as yet; it is too soon, even if she really had genius, but, alas! there appears to be none; all must be done by rule; she has no ideas, and none seem likely to come, for I have tried her in every possible way. Among other things it occurred to me to write out a very simple minuet, and to see if she could not make a variation on it. Well, that utterly failed. Now, thought I, she has not a notion how or what to do first. So I began to vary the first bar, and told her to continue in the same manner, and to keep to the idea. At length this went tolerably well. When it was finished, I told her she must try to originate something herself – only the treble of a melody. So she thought it over for a whole quarter of

121

an hour, and nothing came. Then I wrote four bars of a minuet, saying to her, 'See what an ass I am! I have begun a minuet, and can't even complete the first part; be so very good as to finish it for me.' She declared this was impossible. At last, with great difficulty, something came, and I was only too glad that anything at all came. I told her then to complete the minuet – that is, the treble only. The task I set her for the next lesson was to change my four bars, and replace them by something of her own, and to find out another beginning, even if it were the same harmony, only changing the melody. I shall see tomorrow what she has done...

Maria Anna Mozart to her Husband
Paris, 12 June 1778

My dear Husband,

We received on June 9th your letter of May 28th and were delighted to hear that you were both in good health. Thank God, Wolfgang and I are quite well. I was bled yesterday, so I shan't be able to write much today. Wolfgang is not at home, as he is lunching with Herr Raaff at Count Sickingen's, where they go at least once a week, for Sickingen is devoted to Wolfgang and is himself a great connoisseur of music and composes too. Herr Raaff comes to see us almost every day. He calls me 'Mother', is very fond of us and often spends two or three hours with us. One day he came especially to

sing to me and sang three arias, which gave me great
pleasure. And now whenever he comes to see us he
always sings something to me, for I am quite in love
with his singing. He is a most honourable man and
sincerity itself; if you knew him, you would love him
with all your heart. You want to know where we are
lodging? First of all, find the rue Montmartre and then
the rue Cléry. It is the first street on the left, if you
enter the rue Cléry from the rue Montmartre. It is a
fine street, inhabited almost entirely by the upper
classes, very clean, fairly near the Boulevards, and the
air is healthy. The owners of the house are good, honest
folk and not out to make money, which is unusual in
Paris ...

Leopold Mozart to his Wife and Son
Salzburg, 29 June 1778

My dear Wife, my dear Son!

We trust that you are well. We are both in excellent
health! You will have received my letter of June 11th.
On Holy Trinity Sunday I lunched, as usual, at the
priests' house. In the afternoon Haydn played the organ
during the Litany and the Te Deum, the Archbishop
being present, and he played so abominably that we
were all terrified and thought he was going the way of
Adlgasser of pious memory. But it was only a slight
tipsiness, which made his head and his hands go in

different directions. Since Adlgasser's accident I have
never heard anything like it ...

Mozart to his Father
Paris, 3 July 1778

Monsieur mon très-cher Père,

I have very painful and sad news to give you, which
has, in fact, been the cause of my not having sooner
replied to your letter of the 11th. My dearest mother
is very ill. She has been bled according to her usual
custom, which was indeed very necessary; it did her
much good, but a few days afterwards she complained
of shivering and feverishness; then diarrhœa came on
and headache. At first we only used our home remedies,
antispasmodic powders; we would gladly have had
recourse to the black powder, but we had none, and
could not get it here. As she became every moment
worse, could hardly speak, and lost her hearing, so that
we were obliged to shout to her, Baron Grimm sent his
doctor to see her. She is very weak, and still feverish
and delirious. They do give me some hope, but I have
not much. I hoped and feared alternately day and night
for long, but I am quite reconciled to the will of God,
and hope that you and my sister will be the same. What
other resource have we to make us calm? More calm,
I ought to say; for altogether so we cannot be. Whatever
the result may be, I am resigned, knowing that it comes

from God, who wills all things for our good (however unaccountable they may seem to us); and I do firmly believe (and shall never think otherwise) that no doctor, no man living, no misfortune, no casualty, can either save or take away the life of any human being – none but God alone. These are only the instruments that He usually employs, but not always; we sometimes see people swoon, fall down, and be dead in a moment. When our time does come, all means are vain – they rather hurry on death than retard it; this we saw in the case of our friend Hefner. I do not mean to say by this that my mother will or must die, or that all hope is at an end: she may recover and be restored to health, but only if the Lord wills it thus. After praying to God with all my strength for health and life for my darling mother, I like to indulge in such consolatory thoughts, and, after doing so, I feel more cheerful and more calm and tranquil, and you may easily imagine how much I require comfort. Now for another subject. Let us put aside these sad thoughts, and still hope, but not too much; we must place our trust in the Lord, and console ourselves by the thought that all must go well if it be in accordance with the will of the Almighty, as He knows best what is most profitable and beneficial both for our temporal and spiritual welfare...

Mozart to the Abbé Bullinger, Salzburg

Paris, 3 [actually 4] July 1778

My very dear Friend,

Mourn with me! This has been the most melancholy day of my life; I am now writing at two o'clock in the morning. I must tell you that my mother, my darling mother, is no more. God has called her to Himself; I clearly see that it was His will to take her from us, and I must learn to submit to the will of God. The Lord giveth, and the Lord taketh away. Only think of all the distress, anxiety, and care I have endured for the last fourteen days. She died quite unconscious, and her life went out like a light. She confessed three days before, took the sacrament, and received extreme unction. The last three days, however, she was constantly delirious, and today, at twenty minutes past five o'clock, her features became distorted, and she lost all feeling and perception. I pressed her hand, I spoke to her, but she did not see me, she did not hear me, and all feeling was gone. She lay thus till the moment of her death, five hours after, at twenty minutes past ten at night. There was no one present but myself, Herr Heiner, a kind friend whom my father knows, and the nurse. It is quite impossible for me to describe the whole course of the illness today. I am firmly convinced that she must have died, and that God had so ordained it. All I would ask of you at present is to act the part of a true friend, by preparing my father by degrees for this sad intelligence. I have written to him by this post, but only that she is seriously ill; and now I shall wait for your answer and be guided by it. May God give him strength and courage! My dear friend, I am consoled not only now, but have been so for some time past. By the mercy of God I have borne it all with firmness and composure. When the danger became imminent, I prayed to God for only two things – a happy death for my mother, and strength and courage for myself; and our gracious God heard my prayer and conferred these two boons fully on me. I entreat you, therefore, my best friend, to watch over my father for me; try to inspire him with courage, that the blow may not be too hard and heavy on him when he learns the worst. I also, from my heart, implore you to comfort my sister. Pray go straight to them, but do not tell them she is actually dead – only prepare them for the truth. Do what you think best, say what you please; only act so that my mind may be relieved, and that I may not have to dread another misfortune. Support and comfort my dear father and my dear sister. Answer me at once, I entreat. Adieu! Your faithful

W.A.M.

Mozart to his Father

Paris, 9 July 1778

I hope you are prepared to receive with firmness most
melancholy and painful intelligence. My last letter of
the 3rd must have shown you that no good news could
be hoped for. That very same day, the 3rd, at twenty
minutes past ten at night, my mother fell asleep peacefully in the Lord; indeed, when I wrote to you she was
already in the enjoyment of heavenly bliss, for all was
then over. I wrote to you in the night, and I hope you
and my dear sister will forgive me for this slight but
very necessary deception; for, judging of your grief and
sorrow by my own, I could not prevail on myself to
startle you suddenly by such dreadful intelligence; but
I hope you have now summoned up courage to hear
the worst, and that, after at first giving way to natural,
and only too just, anguish and tears, you will eventually
submit to the will of God, and adore His inscrutable,
unfathomable, and all-wise providence. You can easily
conceive what I have had to endure, and what courage
and fortitude I required to bear with composure seeing
her become daily worse and worse; and yet our gracious
God bestowed this boon on me. I have, indeed, suffered
and wept, but what did it avail? So I strove to be com-
forted, and I do hope, my dear father, that my dear sister
and you will do likewise. Weep, weep, as you cannot fail
to weep, but take comfort at last; remember that God

Almighty has ordained it, and how can we rebel against Him? Let us rather pray to Him and thank Him for His goodness, for she died a happy death. Under these heartrending circumstances there were three things that consoled me – my entire and steadfast submission to the will of God, and the sight of her easy and blessed death, which made me feel that in a moment she had become so happy; for how far happier is she now than we are! Indeed, I would fain at that moment have gone with her. From this wish and longing proceeded my third source of consolation – namely, that she is not lost to us for ever, that we shall see her again, and live together far more happily and blessedly than in this world. The time as yet we know not, but that does not disturb me; when God wills it I am ready. His heavenly and holy will has been fulfilled. Let us therefore pray a pious *Vater unser* for her soul and turn our thoughts to other matters, for there is a time for everything.

I write this in the house of Madame d'Epinay and M. Grimm, with whom I now live; I have a pretty little room with a very agreeable prospect, and am as happy as it is possible to be under my present circumstances. It will be a great aid in restoring my tranquillity, to hear that my dear father and sister submit with calmness and fortitude to the will of God, and trust Him with their whole heart, in the entire belief that He orders all for the best. My dearest father, do not give way! My dearest sister, be firm! You do not as yet know your brother's kind heart, because he has not yet had an opportunity to prove it. Remember, my loved ones both, that you have a son and a brother anxious to devote all his powers to make you happy, knowing well that the day must come when you will not be hostile to his wish and his desire – not certainly such as to be any discredit to him – and that you will do all that lies in your power to make him happy. Oh! then we shall all live together as peacefully, honourably, and contentedly as it is possible to do in this world, and at last in God's good time all meet again above – the purpose for which we were destined and created.

I received your last letter of the 29th, and see with pleasure that you are both, thank God! in good health. I could not help laughing heartily at Haydn's tipsy fit. Had I been there, I certainly should have whispered in his ear 'Adlgasser!' It is really disgraceful in so clever a man to render himself incapable by his own folly of performing his duties at a festival instituted in honour of God; when the Archbishop too and his whole court were present, and the church full of people, it was quite abominable. This is one of my chief reasons for detesting Salzburg – those coarse, slovenly, dissipated court musicians, with whom no honest man of good breeding could possibly live! instead of being glad to associate with them, he must feel ashamed of them. It is probably from this very cause that musicians are neither loved nor respected with us. If the orchestra were only organised like that at Mannheim! I wish you could see the subordination that prevails there – the authority Cannabich exercises; where all is done in earnest. Cannabich, who is the best director I ever saw, is both beloved and feared by his subordinates, who, as well as himself, are respected by the whole town. But certainly they behave very differently, have good manners, are well dressed (and do not go to public-houses to get drunk). This can never be the case in Salzburg, unless the Prince will place confidence either in you or me and give us full powers, which are indispensable to a conductor of music; otherwise it is all in vain. In Salzburg every one is master – so no one is master. If I were to undertake it, I should insist on exercising entire authority. The Grand Chamberlain must have nothing to say as to musical matters, or on any point relating to music. Not every person in authority can become a Capellmeister, but a Capellmeister must become a person of authority...

Mozart to his Father
Paris, 18 July 1778

I hope you got my last two letters. Let us allude no more to their chief purport. All is over; and were we to write whole pages on the subject, we could not alter the fact.

The principal object of this letter is to congratulate my dear sister on her name-day. I think I wrote to you that M. Raaff had left Paris, but that he is my very true and most particular friend, and I can entirely depend on his regard. I could not possibly write to you, because I did not myself know, that he had so much affection for me. Now, to write a story properly, one ought to begin from the beginning. I ought to tell you, first, that Raaff lodged with M. Le Gros. It just occurs to me that you already know this; but what am I to do? It is written, and I can't begin the letter again, so I proceed. When he arrived, we happened to be at dinner. This, too, has nothing to do with the matter; it is only to let you know that people do dine in Paris, as elsewhere. When I went home I found a letter for me from Herr Weber, and the bearer of it was Raaff. If I wished to deserve the name of an historian, I ought here to insert the contents of this letter; and I can with truth say that I am very reluctant to decline giving them. But I must not be too prolix; to be concise is a fine thing, which you can see by my letter. The third day I found him at home and thanked him; it is always advisable to be polite. I no longer remember what we talked about. An historian must be unusually dull who cannot forthwith supply some falsehood – I mean some romance. Well! we spoke of the fine weather; and when we had said our say, we were silent, and I went away. Some days after – though what day it was I really forget, but one day in the week assuredly – I had just seated myself, at the piano of course; and Ritter, the worthy Holzbeisser, was sitting beside me.

Now, what is to be deduced from that? A great deal. Raaff had never heard me at Mannheim except at a concert, where the noise and uproar was so great that nothing could be heard; and *he* had such a miserable piano that I could not have done myself any justice on it. Here, however, the instrument was good, and I saw Raaff sitting opposite me with a speculative air; so, as you may imagine, I played some preludes in the Fischietti method, and also played a florid sonata in the style and with the fire, spirit, and precision of Haydn, and then a fugue with all the skill of Lipp, Silber, and Aman.* My fugue-playing has everywhere gained me the greatest applause. When I had quite finished (Raaff all the time calling out Bravo! while his countenance showed his true and sincere delight), I entered into conversation with Ritter, and among other things said that I by no means liked being here; adding, 'The chief cause of this is music; besides, I can find no resources here, no amusement, no agreeable or sociable inter-course with any one – especially with ladies, many of whom are disreputable, and those who are not so are deficient in good breeding.' Ritter could not deny that I was right. Raaff at last said, smiling, 'I can quite believe it, for M. Mozart is not *wholly* here to admire the Parisian beauties; one half of him is elsewhere – where I have just come from.' This of course gave rise to much

* Fischietti was Capellmeister in Salzburg; Michael Haydn and Lipp, organists.

laughing and joking; but Raaff presently said, in a serious tone, 'You are quite right, and I cannot blame you; she deserves it, for she is a sweet, pretty, good girl, well educated, and a superior person with considerable talent.' This gave me an excellent opportunity strongly to recommend my beloved Madlle. Weber to him; but there was no occasion for me to say much, as he was already quite fascinated by her. He promised me, as soon as he returned to Mannheim, to give her lessons, and to interest himself in her favour . . .

After his mother's death Mozart stayed on in Paris for a further three months but to little avail, and at the beginning of October, after an absence of a year, he started for home – though even then he was unable to resist dragging his heels for another month in Mannheim (much to Leopold's fury). Back in Salzburg he took up the appointment of organist at the cathedral and settled into the old social routine, making up with a vigorous bout of compositional activity for the time that had been wasted in Mannheim and Paris. Then in the summer of 1780 came the commission to write an opera seria for the carnival season in Munich. This was Mozart's biggest opportunity so far, both in itself and for where it might lead, and he seized it with enthusiasm. The subject, chosen by the Munich Court, was Idomeneo, rè di Creta, *and Mozart asked the Court Chaplain of Salzburg, Gianbattista Varesco, to provide him with a libretto. Composition of the music was*

begun in Salzburg but at the beginning of November Mozart
went to Munich and all further collaboration between the
composer and his librettist was conducted by correspondence,
with Leopold Mozart acting as the often rather crusty
intermediary.

Mozart to his Father
Munich, 8 November 1780

Fortunate and pleasant was my arrival here – fortunate, because no mishap occurred during the journey; and pleasant, because we had scarcely patience to wait for the moment that was to end this short but disagreeable journey. I do assure you it was impossible for us to sleep for a moment the whole night. The carriage jolted our very souls out, and the seats were as hard as stone! From Wasserburg I thought I never could arrive in Munich with whole bones, and during two stages I held on by the straps, suspended in the air and not venturing to sit down. But no matter; it is past now, though it will serve me as a warning in future rather to go on foot than drive in a diligence.

Now as to Munich. We arrived here at one o'clock in the forenoon, and the same evening I called on Count Seeau [the Theatre Intendant], but as he was not at home I left a note for him. Next morning I went there with Becke. Seeau has been moulded like wax by the Mannheim people. I have a request to make of the

135

Abbate [Gianbattista Varesco]. The aria of Ilia in the second act and second scene must be a little altered for what I require – '*Se il padre perdei, in te lo ritrovo.*' This verse could not be better; but now comes what always appeared unnatural to me – N.B. in an aria – I mean, to speak aside. In a dialogue these things are natural enough, for a few words can be hurriedly said aside, but in an aria where the words must be repeated it has a bad effect; and even were this not the case, I should prefer an uninterrupted aria. The beginning may remain if he chooses, for it is charming and quite a natural flowing strain, where, not being fettered by the words, I can write on quite easily; for we agreed to bring in an *aria andantino* here in concert with four wind instruments, viz. flute, hautboy, horn, and bassoon, and I beg that you will let me have the air as soon as possible.

Now for a grievance. I have not, indeed, the honour of being acquainted with the hero *Del Prato* [the *musico* who was to sing Idamante], but from description I should say that Cecarelli is rather the better of the two, for often in the middle of an air our *musico*'s breath entirely fails; *nota bene*, he never was on any stage, and Raaff is like a statue. Now only for a moment imagine the scene in the first act! But there is one good thing, which is, that Madame Dorothea Wendling is *arci-contentissima* with her *scena*, and insisted on hearing it played three times in succession. The Grand Master of the Teutonic Order arrived yesterday. 'Essex' was given at the Court Theatre, and a magnificent ballet. The theatre was all illuminated. The beginning was an overture by Cannabich, which, as it is one of his last, I did not know. I am sure, if you had heard it you would have been as much pleased and excited as I was, and if you had not previously known the fact, you certainly could not have believed that it was by Cannabich. Do come soon to hear it, and to admire the orchestra. I have no more to say. There is to be a grand concert this evening, where Mara is to sing three airs. Tell me whether it snows as heavily in Salzburg as here. My kind regards to Herr Schikaneder [*impresario in Salzburg*], and beg him to excuse my not yet sending him the aria, for I have not been able to finish it entirely.

Leopold Mozart to his Son
Salzburg, 11 November 1780

Mon très cher Fils,

I am writing in great haste at half past nine in the evening, as I have had no time all day. Varesco brought me the libretto very late and Count Sepperl Überacker was with us from five o'clock until now.

I am returning the libretto and the draft, so that His Excellency Count Seeau may see that everything has been carried out to order. In about a week a complete copy of the text will follow by the mail coach, showing just how Abbate Varesco wants it to be printed. It will also include the necessary notes. Here is the aria, which is, I think, quite suitable. If not, let me know at once. What you say about the singers is really depressing. Well, your musical composition will have to make up for their deficiencies. I wish I could have heard Madame Mara. Do tell me how she sings. You can imagine that I am looking forward with childish excitement to hearing that excellent orchestra. I only wish that I could get away soon. But I shall certainly not travel by mail coach, for I am rather careful of my two damson stones ...

Mozart to his Father

Munich, 13 November 1780

I write in the greatest haste, for I am not yet dressed, and must go off to Count Seeau's. Cannabich, Quaglio, and Le Grand, the ballet-master, also dine there to consult about what is necessary for the opera. Cannabich and I dined yesterday with Countess Baumgarten,* *née* Lerchenfeld. My friend is all in all in that family, and now I am the same. It is the best and most serviceable house here to me, for owing to their kindness all has gone well with me, and, please God, will continue to do

* He wrote an air for her, the original of which is now in the State Library at Munich.

so. I am just going to dress, but must not omit the chief thing of all, and the principal object of my letter – to wish you, my very dearest and kindest father, every possible good on this your name-day. I also entreat the continuance of your fatherly love, and assure you of my entire obedience to your wishes. Countess la Rosé sends her compliments to you and my sister, so do all the Cannabichs and both Wendling families, Ramm, Eck father and son, Becke, and Herr del Prato, who happens to be with me. Yesterday Count Seeau presented me to the Elector, who was very gracious. If you were to speak to Count Seeau now, you would scarcely recognise him, so completely have the *Mannheimers* transformed him.

I am *ex commissione* to write a formal answer in his name to the Abbate Varesco, but I have no time, and was not born to be a secretary. In the first act (eighth scene) Herr Quaglio made the same objection that we did originally – namely, that it is not fitting the king should be quite alone in the ship. If the Abbé thinks that he can be reasonably represented in the terrible storm forsaken by every one, *without a ship*, exposed to the greatest peril, all may remain as it is; but, N.B., no ship – for he cannot be alone in one; so, if the other mode be adopted, some generals or confidants (mates) must land from the ship with him. Then the king might address a few words to his trusty companions, and desire them to leave him alone, which in his melancholy situation would be quite natural ...

Mozart to his Father

Munich, 15 November 1780

The aria is now admirable, but there is still an alteration
to be made recommended by Raaff; he is, however, right,
and even were he not, some courtesy ought to be shown
to his grey hairs. He was with me yesterday, and I
played over his first aria to him, with which he was very
much pleased. The man is old, and can no longer show
off in an aria like that in the second act – *'Fuor del mar
hò un mare in seno,'* &c. As, moreover, in the third act he
has no aria (the one in the first act not being so *cantabile*
as he would like, owing to the expression of the words),
he wishes after his last speech, *'O Creta fortunata, O me
felice,'* to have a pretty aria to sing instead of the quar-
tett; in this way a superfluous air would be got rid of,
and the third act produce a far better effect. In the last
scene also of the second act, Idomeneo has an aria, or
rather a kind of cavatina, to sing between the choruses.
For this it would be better to substitute a mere recitative, well supported by the instruments. For in this
scene (owing to the action and grouping which have
been recently settled with Le Grand), the finest of the
whole opera, there cannot fail to be such a noise and
confusion in the theatre, that an aria would make a very
bad figure in this place, and moreover there is a thun-
derstorm which is not likely to subside during Raaff's
aria! The effect, therefore, of a recitative between the

choruses must be infinitely better. Lisel Wendling has also sung through her two arias half a dozen times, and is much pleased with them. I heard from a third person that the two Wendlings highly praised their arias, and as for Raaff he is my best and dearest friend. I must teach the whole opera myself to Del Prato. He is incapable of singing even the introduction to any air of importance, and his voice is so uneven! He is only engaged for a year, and at the end of that time (next September) Count Seeau will get another. Cecarelli might try his chance then *sérieusement.*

I nearly forgot the best of all. After mass last Sunday Count Seeau presented me, *en passant*, to H. S. H. the Elector, who was very gracious. He said, 'I am happy to see you here again'; and on my replying that I would strive to deserve the good opinion of His Serene Highness, he clapped me on the shoulder, saying, 'Oh! I have no doubt whatever that all will go well – *a piano piano si và lontano.'*

Deuce take it! I cannot write everything I wish. Raaff has just left me; he sends you his compliments, and so do the Cannabichs, and Wendlings, and Ramm. My sister must not be idle, but practise steadily, for every one is looking forward with pleasure to her coming here. My lodging is in the Burggasse at M. Fiat's [where the marble slab to his memory is now erected].

Mozart to his Father
Munich, 22 November 1780

I send herewith, at last, the long-promised aria for Herr Schikaneder. During the first week that I was here I could not entirely complete it, owing to the business that caused me to come here. Besides, Le Grand, the ballet-master, a terrible talker and bore, has just been with me, and by his endless chattering caused me to miss the diligence. I hope my sister is quite well. I have at this moment a bad cold, which in such weather is quite the fashion here. I hope and trust, however, that it will soon take its departure – indeed, both phlegm and cough are gradually disappearing. In your last letter you write repeatedly, 'Oh! my poor eyes! I do not wish to write myself blind – half-past eight at night, and no spectacles!' But why do you write at night, and without spectacles? I cannot understand it. I have not yet had an opportunity of speaking to Count Seeau, but hope to do so today, and shall give you any information I can gather by the next post. At present all will, no doubt, remain as it is. Herr Raaff paid me a visit yesterday morning, and I gave him your regards, which seemed to please him much. He is, indeed, a worthy and thoroughly respectable man. The day before yesterday Del Prato sang in the most disgraceful way at the concert. I would almost lay a wager that the man never manages to get through the rehearsals, far less the opera; he has some internal disease.

Come in! – Herr Panzacchi! [who was to sing Arbace]. He has already paid me three visits, and has just asked me to dine with him on Sunday. I hope the same thing won't happen to me that happened to us with the coffee. He meekly asks if, instead of *se la sà*, he may sing *se co là*, or even *ut, re, mi, fa, sol, là*.

I am so glad when you often write to me, only not at night, and far less without spectacles. You must, however, forgive me if I do not say much in return, for every minute is precious; besides, I am obliged chiefly to write at night, for the mornings are so very dark; then I have to dress, and the servant at the Weiser sometimes admits a troublesome visitor. When Del Prato comes I must sing to him, for I have to teach him his whole part like a child; his method is not worth a farthing. I will write more fully next time. What of the family portraits? My sister, if she has nothing better to do, might mark down the names of the best comedies that have been performed during my absence. Has Schikaneder still good receipts? My compliments to all my friends, and to Gilofsky's Katherl. Give a pinch of Spanish snuff from me to Bimperl [the dog], a good wine-sop, and three kisses. Do you not miss me at all? A thousand compliments to all – all! Adieu! I embrace you both from my heart, and hope my sister will soon recover. [Nannerl, partly owing to her grief in consequence of an unfortunate love-affair, was suffering from pains in the chest, which threatened to turn to consumption.]

Mozart to his Father
Munich, 1 December 1780

The rehearsal went off with extraordinary success; there were only six violins in all, but the requisite wind instruments. No one was admitted but Count Seeau's sister and young Count Seinsheim. This day week we are to have another rehearsal with twelve violins for the first act, and then the second act will be rehearsed (like the first on the previous occasion). I cannot tell you how delighted and surprised all were; but I never expected anything else, for I declare I went to this rehearsal with as quiet a heart as if I had been going to a banquet. Count Seinsheim said to me, 'I do assure you that though I expected a great deal from you, I can truly say this I did not expect.'

The Cannabichs and all who frequent their house are true friends of mine. After the rehearsal (for we had a great deal to discuss with the Count) when I went home with Cannabich, Madame Cannabich came to meet me, and hugged me from joy at the rehearsal having passed off so admirably; then came Ramm and Lang, quite out of their wits with delight. My true friend the excellent lady, who was alone in the house with her invalid daughter Rose, had been full of solicitude on my account. When you know him, you will find Ramm a true German, saying exactly what he thinks to your face. He said to me, 'I must honestly confess that no music ever made such an impression on me, and I assure you I thought of your father fifty times at least, and of the joy he will feel when he hears this opera.' But enough of this subject. My cold is rather worse owing to this rehearsal, for it is impossible not to feel excited when honour and fame are at stake, however cool you may be at first. I did everything you prescribed for my cold, but it goes on very slowly, which is particularly inconvenient to me at present; but all my writing about it will not put an end to my cough, and yet write I must. Today I have begun to take violet syrup and a little almond oil, and already I feel relieved, and have again stayed two days in the house. Yesterday morning Herr Raaff came to me again to hear the aria in the second act. The man is as much enamoured of his aria, as a young passionate lover ever was of his fair one. He sings it the last thing before he goes to sleep, and the first thing in the morning when he awakes. I knew already, from a sure source, but now from himself, that he said to Herr von Viereck (Oberststallmeister) and to Herr von Kastel, 'I am accustomed constantly to change my parts, to suit me better, in recitative as well as in arias, but this I have left just as it was, for every single note is in accordance with my voice.' In short, he is as happy as a king. He wishes the interpolated aria to be a little altered, and so do I. The part commencing with the word *era* he does not like, for what we want here is a calm tranquil aria; and if consisting of only one part, so much the better, for a second subject would have to be brought in about the middle, which leads me out of my way. In 'Achill in Sciro' there is an air of this kind, '*or che mio figlio sei*'. I thank my sister very much for the list of comedies she sent me. It is singular enough about the comedy 'Rache für Rache'; it was frequently given here with much applause, and quite lately too, though I was not there myself. I beg you will present my devoted homage to Madlle. Therèse von Barisani; if I had a brother, I would request him to kiss her hand in all humility, but having a sister only is still better, for I beg she will embrace her in the most affectionate manner in my name. *A propos*, do write a letter to Cannabich; he deserves it, and it will please him exceedingly. What does it matter if he does not answer you? You must not judge him from his manner; he is the same to every one, and means nothing. You must first know him well.

Leopold Mozart to his Son
Salzburg, 4 December 1780

... I have just been to see Varesco. As your letter of December 1st arrived while I was out, your sister read it, looked up the passage in Metastasio, and sent the letter and the book after me to Varesco's. All

that you have pointed out shall be done. You know that
I too thought the subterranean speech too long. I have given
Varesco my candid opinion and it will now be made
as short as possible. We are delighted to hear that the
rehearsal went so well. I have no doubt whatever nor
am I the slightest bit anxious about your work, provided
the production is good, I mean, *provided there are good
people to perform it* – and that is the case in Munich.
So I am not at all worried; but when your music is
performed by a mediocre orchestra, it will always be
the loser, because it is composed with so much discern-
ment for the various instruments and is far from being
commonplace, as, on the whole, Italian music is. That
your cold should have become worse after the rehearsal
is only natural, for, owing to the concentration upon
hearing and seeing, all the nerves of the head become
excited and strained, and eagerness and attention
extends this tension to the chest also ...

Mozart to his Father
Munich, 5 December 1780

The death of the Empress [Maria Theresa] does not at
all affect my opera, for the theatrical performances are
not suspended, and the plays go on as usual. The entire
mourning is not to last more than six weeks, and my
opera will not be given before the 20th of January. I wish
you to get my black suit thoroughly brushed to make it

as wearable as possible, and forward it to me by the first diligence; for next week every one must be in mourning, and I, though constantly on the move, must cry with the others.

Leopold Mozart to his Son
Salzburg, 9 December 1780

... Here is the suit, such as it is. I had to have it patched quickly, for the whole taffeta lining of the waistcoat was in rags. I am writing this letter on Saturday, December 9th, at half past nine in the evening. Herr Esser gave a concert in the theatre today and actually made a profit of forty gulden. He will arrive in Munich by this diligence and will call on you at once. He is a bit of an idiot. But he plays (when he plays *seriously*) with the *surest and most astounding execution.* At the same time he has a *beautiful adagio,* which few good allegro-players possess. But when he starts playing the fool, he plays on the G-string only and with the greatest skill and technique. By striking his strings with a wooden pencil he performs whole pieces with amazing rapidity and precision. He plays the viola d'amore charmingly. But what touched me and struck me at first as rather childish was his *whistling.* He whistles recitatives and arias as competently as any singer and with the most perfect expression, introducing portamento, flourishes, trills and so on, most admirably, and all the time accompanying himself pizzicato on the violin. He came to see us every day *and drank like a fish*. This great talent of his brings him in a good deal of money – *and yet he never has any cash*.

Addio. We both kiss you. I shall write to you again on Monday. Farewell. I am your faithful father

MZT

You will find the two trumpet mutes packed with the suit.

Leopold Mozart to his Son
Salzburg, 11 December 1780

... I enclose a note from Varesco and also the aria. Act I with the translation and possibly Act II will arrive in Munich next week by the mail coach. I trust that you are well. I advise you when composing to consider not only the musical, but also *the unmusical public*. You must remember that to every ten real connoisseurs there are a *hundred ignoramuses*. So do not neglect the so-called *popular* style, which tickles *long ears*. What about the score? Are you not going to have it copied? You must think over what you are going to do and *you must make some sensible arrangement*. The remuneration you are getting *is so small that you really cannot leave your score behind*. Farewell. Give our greetings to all, just as all here send their greetings to you. We kiss you millions of times and I am your honest old father

L. MZT

Do not hurry over Act III. You will certainly be ready in time.

All's well that ends well!

Mozart to his Father
Munich, 19 December 1780

Mon très cher Père!

I have received safely the last aria for Raaff (who sends greetings to you), the two trumpet mutes, your letter of the 15th, and the pair of socks. The second rehearsal went off as well as the first. The orchestra and the whole audience discovered to their delight that the second act was actually more expressive and original than the first. Next Saturday both acts are to be rehearsed again. But this time the rehearsal is to be held in a large hall at Court, and this I have long wished for, because there is not nearly enough room at Count Seeau's. The Elector is to listen incognito in an adjoining room. Well, as Cannabich said to me, 'We shall have to rehearse like the deuce.' At the last rehearsal he was dripping with sweat ...

A propos – now for the most important thing of all – for I must hurry. I hope to receive by the next mail coach the first act at least, together with the translation. The scene between father and son in Act I and the first scene in Act II between Idomeneo and Arbace are both too long. They would certainly bore the audience, particularly as in the first scene both the actors are bad, and in the second, one of them is; besides, they only contain a narrative of what the spectators have already seen with their own eyes. These scenes are being printed as they stand. But I should like the Abbate to indicate how they may be shortened – and as drastically as possible, – for otherwise I shall have to shorten them myself. These two scenes cannot remain as they are – I mean, when set to music ...

Leopold Mozart to his Son
Salzburg, 25 December 1780

The whole town is talking about the excellence of your opera. Baron Lehrbach spread the first report. The Court Chancellor's wife tells me that he told her that your opera was being praised to the skies. The second report was set going by Herr Becke's letter to Fiala, which the latter made everyone read. I should like Act III to produce the same effect. I feel certain that it will, the more so as in this act great passions are expressed and the subterranean voice will undoubtedly astonish and terrify. Basta, I trust that people will say: *Finis coronat opus.* But do your best to keep the whole orchestra in good humour; flatter them, and, by praising them, keep them all in your favour. For I know your style of composition – it requires unusually close attention from the players of every type of instrument;

and to keep the whole orchestra at such a pitch of industry and alertness for at least three hours is no joke. Each performer, even the least important viola-player, is deeply touched by personal praise and becomes much more zealous and attentive, while a little courtesy of this kind only costs you a word or two. However – you know all this yourself – I am just mentioning it, because rehearsals afford few opportunities to do this, and so it is forgotten; and when the opera is staged, one really needs the cordial support and enthusiasm of the whole orchestra. Their position is then quite different, and the attention of every single performer must be tested even further. You know that you cannot count on the goodwill of everyone, for there is always *an undercurrent of doubt and questioning*. People wondered whether Act II would be as new and excellent as Act I. As this doubt has now been removed, few will have any doubts as to Act III. But I will wager my head that there are some who are wondering whether *your music will produce the same effect in a theatre as it does in a room*. And here you really need the greatest goodwill on the part of the whole body of players ...

Leopold Mozart to his Son
Salzburg, 29 December 1780

... God be praised that His Highness is satisfied with the first two acts, or rather is thoroughly delighted. I daresay that when your opera is staged, you will have many more points to raise, particularly in Act III, where there is so much action.

I assume that you will choose very deep wind-instruments to accompany the subterranean voice. How would it be if after the slight subterranean rumble the instruments *sustained, or rather began to sustain, their notes piano and then made a crescendo such as might well inspire terror, while after this and during the decrescendo the voice would begin to sing*? And there might be a terrifying crescendo at *every phrase uttered by the voice.* Owing to the rumble, which must be short, and rather like the shock of a thunderbolt, which sends up the figure of Neptune, the attention of the audience is aroused; and this attention is intensified by the introduction of a quiet, prolonged and then swelling and very agitating wind-instrument passage, and finally becomes strained to the utmost when, behold! *a voice* is heard. Why, I seem to see and hear it.

It was a good thing to have your suit turned. Now that we are discussing clothes, *I suppose I can save myself the trouble of bringing my braided suit. You know that I do not care about dressing up.* Please let me know about this ...

Mozart to his Father

Munich, 3 January 1781

My head and my hands are so fully occupied with my
third act, that it would not be wonderful if I turned into
a third act myself, for it alone has cost me more trouble
than the entire opera; there is scarcely a scene in it
which is not interesting to the greatest degree. The
accompaniment of the underground music consists
merely of five instruments, namely, three trombones
and two French horns, which are placed on the spot
whence the voice proceeds. The whole orchestra is
silent at this part.

The grand rehearsal positively takes place on the
20th, and the first performance on the 22nd. All you
will both require is to bring one black dress, and another
for everyday wear, when you are only visiting intimate
friends where there is no ceremony, and thus save your
black dress a little; and if my sister likes, one pretty
dress also, that she may go to the ball and the Académie
Masquée . . .

Leopold Mozart to his Son

Salzburg, 4 January 1781

Mon très cher Fils!

I received your letter of December 30th at nine
o'clock, just as I was going to the service. After Church

I did my New Year *seccature* and then went to see Varesco at half past ten. He was horribly angry and said the most foolish things, as Italians or half-Italians do. He mentioned among other things that he had written a few days ago to Count Seeau asking him to see that there would be no misprints in the text; good! that he would like to have twelve copies; basta! that he hoped to receive a few more ducats in recognition of the fact that he had copied the text four times and subsequently had had to make a good many alterations: and that, if he had known beforehand, he would not have agreed to write the text for the small remuneration of twenty ducats. *As far as I am concerned, it was a good move.* But I immediately began to think that the godless Italian idea might occur to Varesco that *we had made a better bargain and were keeping the money* ... I listened to him in complete silence and when at last I got tired of his railing and his silly chatter, I said to him: '*The only reply I want is whether or not I am to write today to say that next post-day, January 4th, another aria will be sent to Munich. For reply I must! The rest does not concern me in the very least.*' He then said: '*I will see whether anything occurs to me.*' So I went off to finish my New Year *seccature.* You can gather from the remarks he has jotted down beside the aria what else he said and how enraged he was ...

Mozart to his Father

Munich, 18 January 1781

Pray forgive a short letter, for I must go this very
moment, ten o'clock (in the forenoon of course), to the
rehearsal. There is to be a recitative rehearsal for the
first time today in the theatre. I could not write before,
having been so incessantly occupied with those con-
founded dances. *Laus Deo*, I have got rid of them at last,
but only of what was most pressing. The rehearsal of
the third act went off admirably. It was considered very
superior to the second act. The poetry is, however,
thought far too long, and of course the music likewise
(which I always said it was). On this account the aria of
Idamante, '*Nò la morte io non pavento*', is to be omitted,
which was, indeed, always out of place there; those who
have heard it with the music deplore this. Raaff's last
air, too, is still more regretted, but we must make a
virtue of necessity. The prediction of the oracle is still
far too long, so I have shortened it; but Varesco need
know nothing of this, because it will all be printed just
as he wrote it. Madame von Robinig will bring with her
the payment both for him and Schachtner. Herr
Geschwender declined taking any money with him. In
the meantime say to Varesco in my name, that he will
not get a farthing from Count Seeau beyond the contract, for all the alterations were made *for me* and not
for the Count, and he ought to be obliged to me into the

156

bargain, as they were indispensable for his own reputation. There is a good deal that might still be altered; and I can tell him that he would not have come off so well with any other composer as with me. I have spared no trouble in defending him.

The stove is out of the question, for it costs too much. I will have another bed put up in the room that adjoins the alcove, and we must manage the best way we can. Do not forget to bring my little watch with you. We shall probably make an excursion to Augsburg, where we could have the little silly thing regulated. I wish you also to bring Schachtner's operetta. There are people who frequent Cannabich's house, who might as well hear a thing of the kind. I must be off to the rehearsal. Adieu!

After the performances of Idomeneo *Mozart overstayed his leave in Munich, and in March 1781 was summoned peremptorily to Vienna by the Archbishop of Salzburg, who had gone there on an extended visit with his entire Court and required the presence of his young employee to help in the entertainment of his guests. But relations between prelate and composer worsened rapidly and within three months Mozart at last found himself a free agent, alone and (to his father's evident apprehension) independent for the first time in his life. Though he didn't know it, he was never to live in Salzburg again.*

Mozart to his Father
Vienna, 17 March 1781

Yesterday, the 16th, I am happy to say I arrived here all alone in a post-chaise. I forgot to mention the hour – 9 o'clock in the morning. I reached St. Pölten on Thursday evening at seven o'clock, as tired as a dog, slept till two o'clock in the morning, and then proceeded direct to Vienna. Where do you think I am writing this? In Mesmer's garden in the Landstrasse. The old lady is not at home; but Fräulein Fränzl is now Frau von Lensch. Upon my word, I should scarcely have known her, she is grown so stout and fat. She has three children (two girls and a boy). One of the girls is named Nannerl; she is four years old, but looks like six; the young gentleman is three, and looks like seven; and the child of nine months might be taken for two years old – they are all so strong, and robust, and well-grown. Now as to the Archbishop. I have a charming room in his house; Brunetti and Cecarelli lodge in another – *che distinzione!* My neighbour is Herr von Kleinmayrn, who, on my arrival, loaded me with all sorts of civilities, and really is a charming man. We dine at eleven o'clock in the forenoon, unluckily rather too early an hour for me. Our party consists of the two valets, the Comptroller, Herr Zetti the confectioner, the two cooks, Cecarelli, Brunetti, and my insignificant self. – N.B. The two valets sit at the head of the table. I have, at all events, the honour to be placed above the cooks; I almost believe I am back in Salzburg! At table all kinds of coarse silly joking go on; but no one jokes with me, for I never say a word, or, if I am obliged to speak, I do so with the utmost gravity, and when I have dined I go away. There is no supper-table at night, but we each receive three ducats, so we cannot be very prodigal. The Archbishop is so good as to add to his lustre by his household, whom he prevents earning their living, and yet never pays them an equivalent. Yesterday, at four o'clock, we had music; at least twenty persons of the highest rank were present. Cecarelli had previously sung at Palfi's. We are to go today to Prince Gallitzin's, who was at the Archbishop's yesterday. I shall now wait to see whether I receive any remuneration; if not, I mean to go to the Archbishop and say to him, in a straightforward manner, that if he does not choose that I should gain my own livelihood, he must supply me with money, for I cannot live on my own means. I must now conclude, as I intend to post this letter myself in passing, for I am going now to Prince Gallitzin's.

P.S. – I went to see the Fischers; I cannot describe their joy. The whole family desire to be remembered to you. I hear that they are giving concerts at Salzburg. What a terrible loss for me! Adieu! My address is, 'Im Deutschen Hause, Singerstrasse'.

Mozart to his Father

Vienna, 8 April 1781

... What you write as to my presence contributing to
the vanity of the Archbishop is in so far just; but of what
use is that to me? I cannot subsist on it. Believe me, I am
right in saying that here he serves only as a *screen* to me.
What distinction, pray, does he confer on me? Herr von
Kleinmayrn and Bönike have a table apart with the illustrious Count Arco. It would be a distinction were I at
this table; but not where I now am with the valets, who,
when not occupying *the first seats at table*, light the
lustres, open the doors, and wait in the ante-room (*when
I am within*), and with cooks too! If we are summoned
to any house where there is a concert, Herr Angerbauer
has orders to watch outside, and when the Salzburg
gentlemen arrive, he then calls a lacquey to precede
them that they may enter. On hearing Brunetti mention
this in the course of conversation, I thought to myself,
only wait till it is my turn! So the other day, when we
were desired to go to Prince Gallitzin's, Brunetti said
to me, in his usual polite manner, 'You must be here this
evening at seven o'clock, that we may go together to
Prince Gallitzin's. Angerbauer will take us there.'
I answered, 'Very well; but if I am not here exactly at
seven o'clock, pray proceed there yourself, and don't
wait for me. I know where to find you; and we are sure
to see each other at the concert.' I purposely went alone,

because I really feel ashamed to go about with him. When I arrived, I found Angerbauer waiting to direct the lacquey to show me in. I, however, took no notice either of Angerbauer or the lacquey, but passed straight on through the rooms into the concert-room (all the doors being open), and going up at once to the Prince I made him my bow, and then remained standing and conversing with him. I had totally forgotten my friends Brunetti and Cecarelli, for they were nowhere to be seen, inasmuch as they were leaning on the wall hidden behind the orchestra, not daring to move a step in advance. If a lady or a gentleman speaks to Cecarelli, he always laughs; and if any one addresses Brunetti, he colours and gives the shortest possible reply. Oh! I should have plenty to write about, if I cared to describe all the scenes that have occurred since I came here with the Archbishop and Cecarelli and Brunetti. I only wonder that he is not ashamed of Brunetti; but I am, instead of him. The fellow, too, dislikes being here, for the whole thing is on too noble a scale for his taste, except at dinner, which is his happiest hour. Prince Gallitzin asked Cecarelli to sing today; next time, I suppose, my turn will come. I am going this evening with Herr von Kleinmayrn to one of his intimate friends, Councillor Braun, whom we all consider to be one of the greatest enthusiasts here for the piano. I have dined twice with Countess Thun and go to see her almost every day. I do think she is the most charming and lovely person I ever saw in my life; and she has also a high opinion of me. Her husband is just the same singular but well-meaning honourable man that he always was. I also dined with Count Cobenzl. I owe this to his aunt, Countess von Rumbeck, sister of Cobenzl in the Pagerie, who was in Salzburg with her husband.

My chief object here is to find my way in a becoming manner into the presence of the Emperor, for I am quite resolved that he shall *know me*. It would be a great pleasure to me to play over my opera to him, and then a lot of fugues, for these are his chief favourites. Oh! if I had only known that I was to be in Vienna at Easter, I would have written a short oratorio, and had it performed in the theatre for my benefit, as this is what every one does here. I should have found no difficulty in writing it previously, as I know all the voices here. How gladly would I give a public concert, which is customary in Vienna; but I know, only too well, that I could not obtain permission to do so. For just imagine! You are aware that there is a society here which gives concerts for the benefit of the widows of musicians, where every professional musician plays *gratis*. The orchestra is a hundred and eighty strong. No virtuoso, with any love for his neighbour, refuses to give his services when the society applies to him; besides, in this way popularity is gained both with the Emperor and with the public. Starzer was commissioned to ask me to play, to which I at once agreed, but said I must first take the good pleasure of my Prince on the subject; but that I had no doubt whatever of his consent, as it was an occasion worthy the support of the Church, and I was not to receive money but merely to perform a good work. *He would not permit it.* All the nobility here have taken this highly amiss. I regret it, because I did not intend to have played any concerto (as the Emperor was to be in the proscenium box), but as Countess Thun was to lend me her fine Stein pianoforte, I would have first extemporised a fugue, and then played the variations on 'Je suis Lindor'. Whenever I have done so in public, I have gained the greatest applause, as there is such a contrast between each variation, and because each has its merit. But *pazienza!* Fiala stands at least two thousand times higher in my opinion for refusing to play for less than a ducat. Has my sister not yet been asked to perform? I hope she will ask two ducats, for as we have always been so different from the rest of the court musicians, I trust we shall be so on this occasion also. If they don't want her they may let it alone; but if they do, they must pay the money. *A propos*, what of the present from the Elector? Has he sent anything yet? Were you at Baumgarten's before you left? . . .

Mozart to his Father
Vienna, 8 April 1781

I began an interesting long letter to you, but I wrote too much about Brunetti in it, and was afraid that his curiosity might tempt him to open the letter, because Cecarelli is with me. I will send it by the next post, and write more fully than I can today. I wrote to you about the applause in the theatre, but I must add that what most of all delighted and surprised me was the extraordinary silence, and also the cries of bravo! while I was playing. This is certainly honour enough in Vienna, where there are such numbers and numbers of good pianists. Today (for I am writing at eleven at night) we had a concert, where three of my pieces were performed – new ones, of course. The Rondo of a concerto for Brunetti, a sonata for myself, with violin accompaniment, which I composed last night between eleven and twelve o'clock, but in order to have it ready in time, I only wrote out the accompaniment for Brunetti, and retained my own part in my head. The third was a rondo for Cecarelli, which was encored. I must now beg you to send me a letter as soon as possible, and to give me your fatherly and friendly advice on the following point. It is reported that we are to return to Salzburg a fortnight hence; by remaining here, I not only do myself no injury, but must derive benefit from it. I have, therefore, some intention of asking the Archbishop's permission to stay on here. Dearest father, I love you truly, which is proved by my renouncing for your sake my every wish and desire; for, were it not on your account, I give you my honour that I would not hesitate for a moment to give up my situation. I would announce a grand concert, take pupils, and, in the course of a twelvemonth, prosper so much in Vienna that I could make an income of 1,000 thalers. I assure you it often weighs on my mind heavily enough that I should thus throw away my luck. I am still young, as you say. True – but to squander one's youth away in such a beggarly place in inactivity is really too sad, besides being uprofitable also. I therefore entreat your kind and paternal counsel about this, and soon too, for I must decide. Above all, place confidence in me, for I think more prudently now. Farewell!

Mozart to his Father
Vienna, 9 May 1781

I am still filled with the gall of bitterness; and I feel sure that you, my good kind father, will sympathise with me. My patience has been so long tried that it has at last given way. I have no longer the misfortune to be in the Salzburg service, and today is a happy day for me.

Three times already has this – I know not what to call him – said the most insulting and impertinent things to my face, which I did not repeat to you, from the wish to spare your feelings, and I only refrained from taking my revenge on the spot because I always had you, my dear father, before my eyes. He called me a knave and a dissolute fellow, and told me to take myself off. And I endured it all, though I felt that not only my own honour but yours was aggrieved by this; but as you would have it so, I was silent. Now hear what passed. Eight days ago the messenger came to me quite unexpectedly, and said I must instantly leave my lodgings. Due notice had been given to the others, but not to me. I packed up my things hurriedly, and old Madame Weber* was so kind as to take me into her house, where I have a pretty room, and am with obliging people, ready to supply me at once with all that I require (not so easy to procure when quite alone). I fixed my journey for Wednesday 9th (this very day) with the post-carriage. Not being able, however, in the interim to collect the money I have yet to receive, I postponed my journey till Saturday. When I went to the Archbishop today, the valet told me that the Prince meant to give me a packet to take charge of. I asked whether it was pressing, on which he said yes, that it was of great importance. 'Then I regret that I cannot have the honour of being of use to his Highness on this occasion; for, owing to particular reasons (which I mentioned), I am not to leave this till Saturday. I am no longer living in this house, and must pay my own way, so it is evident that I cannot set off till

*Aloysia being engaged at the court theatre, the family were in Vienna; but the father was now dead.

I have the means of doing so; for surely no one can wish me to be a loser.' Kleinmayrn, Moll, Brunetti, and the two valets, all said I was quite right. When I went in to the Archbishop – [N.B., I must tell you that Schlauka, one of the valets, advised me to make the excuse that the post-carriage was full, for that would be a valid reason in his eyes – when I entered the room], the first thing he said was, 'Well! when are you going, young fellow?' I replied, 'I intended to have gone tonight, but every place in the post-carriage is already engaged.' Then came all in a breath that I was the most dissipated fellow he knew, no man served him so badly as I did, and he recommended me to set off the same day, or else he would write home to stop my salary. It was impossible to get in a syllable, for his words blazed away like a fire. I heard it all with calmness; he actually told me to my face the deliberate falsehood, that I had a salary of 500 florins – called me a ragamuffin, a scamp, a rogue. Oh! I really cannot write all he said. At last my blood began to boil, and I said, 'Your Grace does not appear to be satisfied with me.' 'How! do you dare to threaten me, you rascal? There is the door, and I tell you I will have nothing more to do with such a low fellow!' At last I said, 'Nor I with you.' 'Begone!' said he; while I replied, as I left the room, 'The thing is settled, and you shall have it tomorrow in writing.' I put it to you, my dear father, if I was not rather too late in saying this than too soon. My honour is more precious to me than all

167

else, and I know it is the same to you. Be under no anxiety on my account; I am so sure of success here, that for a much less cause I would have given up my situation. I have, besides, three different times had good reason to do so, till such treatment seemed to become quite a matter of course. I was twice called a cowardly fellow, so I was resolved not to deserve the name a third time ...

Mozart to his Father
Vienna, 15 May 1781

You know by my last letter that I have demanded a formal dismission from the Prince, as in fact he himself discharged me. Indeed, in my first two audiences he said to me, 'If you can't serve me better, you may go about your business.' He will no doubt deny it, but it is as true as that there is a Providence above. Is it then surprising that at last (irritated to madness by such respectable epithets in the mouth of a Prince as rogue, rascal, raga-muffin, base fellow), the 'take yourself off' should have been accepted by me in its literal sense? Next day I brought Count Arco a memorial to present to the Archbishop, and also returned to him the money for my travelling expenses, consisting of 15 florins and 40 kreuzers for the diligence, and two ducats for my board. He refused to accept either, and declared that I had not the power to throw up my situation without your consent. He said, 'This is your duty.' I replied that

I knew my duty towards my father as well, and perhaps better than he did, and I should very much regret were I obliged to learn it from him. 'Very well,' he replied; 'if he is satisfied, you can request your discharge, and if not – why, you can ask for it all the same.' A fine distinction! All the edifying things that the Archbishop had said to me in the last three audiences, especially in the last, and the pious epithets this admirable man of God applied to me afresh, had such an effect on my bodily frame, that the same evening at the opera I was obliged to go home in the middle of the first act in order to lie down, for I was very feverish, trembled in every limb, and staggered in the street like a drunken man. I stayed in the house both the following day and yesterday, and passed the whole forenoon in bed, having taken tamarind water. The Count was so friendly as to write all sorts of fine things about me to his father, which probably you have been obliged to gulp down. His letter no doubt contains many fabulous passages, but those who write comedies must somewhat exaggerate if they wish to gain applause, and not adhere too closely to actual truth; and you cannot fail to appreciate the officiousness of this gentleman! Without flying into a passion, for I have too much regard for my health and life to do so (it pains me enough when I am forced to it), I will now tell you the chief reproach brought against my service. I did not know that I was a valet, and this was my ruin. I ought to have loitered every morning for a couple of hours in the anteroom. Indeed, I was often told that I ought to show myself more, but somehow I never could understand that it was part of my duty, so I only came punctually when the Archbishop summoned me.

I confide to you briefly my unalterable resolution, but still the whole world is welcome to hear it. If the Archbishop of Salzburg were to offer me a salary of 2,000 florins and any other person 1,000, I would accept the latter, because with the 1,000 I should enjoy health and peace of mind. By all the fatherly love you have invariably shown me since my childhood, and for which I never through life can be sufficiently grateful (though less so in Salzburg than elsewhere), I adjure you, as you wish to see your son enjoy health and happiness, not to write to me any more on the subject, but to bury it in the most profound oblivion, for one word more would suffice to rouse both my spleen and yours. You must yourself own this. Now farewell!

Mozart to his Father
Vienna, 12 May 1781

In the letter I sent by post, I wrote as if we were in the presence of the Archbishop, but now I am going to talk to you, dearest father, quite confidentially. Let us say nothing whatever of all the injustice with which the Archbishop has treated me from the very beginning of his reign to the present moment, of his incessant abuse, of all the impertinences and insults which he lavished on me to my face, nor of the undeniable right I have to leave him, for it cannot be denied. But I wish to speak of what would have induced me to leave him, even without any cause of offence. I have here the best and most useful acquaintances in the world; I am beloved and esteemed by the highest families; I am treated with every possible consideration, and well paid into the bargain; and am I to pine away my life in Salzburg for the sake of 400 florins, to linger on without remuneration or encouragement, and unable to benefit you, which I shall certainly have it in my power to do here? What would be the result? Ever and always the same – I must either fret myself to death, or again go away. I need say no more, for you know it yourself. But this I must tell you, that every one in Vienna has heard the story, and all the nobility take my part, and say that I ought no longer to allow myself to be defrauded in this manner. Dearest father, no doubt they will try to beguile you by many kind words, but these people are snakes and vipers; all base souls are so – disgustingly proud, and yet always ready to crawl. How odious! The two valets know the whole obnoxious affair, and Schlauka in particular said to some one, 'As for me, I really cannot say that I think Mozart wrong – in fact, I think he is quite right. Only suppose the Archbishop had treated me in such a way! He spoke to him as if he had been some miserable beggar. I heard it all – infamous!' The Archbishop acknowledges his injustice, but has he not had frequent cause to do so? and has he ever behaved better in consequence? Never! So let us have done with it. If I had not been afraid of perhaps injuring you, things should long since have been on a very different footing; but, in fact, what can he do to you? – nothing! When you know that all is going well with me, you can easily dispense with the Archbishop's favour. He cannot deprive you of your salary; besides, you always do your duty. I pledge myself to succeed, or I never would have taken this step, although I must confess to you that after such an insult I would have quitted his service, even if forced to beg my bread. For who would submit to be bullied, more especially when you can do far better? In the meantime, if you are afraid, pretend to be displeased with me, scold me well in your letters, and we two alone will know how the matter really stands; but do not allow yourself to be misled by flattery – be on your guard. By the next opportunity I shall send you the portrait, the ribbons, and the lawn. Adieu!

Mozart to his Father
Vienna, 19 May 1781

I really don't know how or what to write, my dearest father, for I have not yet recovered from my astonishment, and never shall if you persist in thinking and writing as you do. I must confess that I do not recognise one feature of my father in your letter! A father, indeed – but not a kind loving father, concerned for the honour of his children and his own – in short, not *my* father. But it must have been a dream. You are now once more awake, and require no reply to your observations to be fully convinced that I shall *now more than ever* abide by my decision. Still, as my honour and my character are so grievously assailed in various quarters, I must allude to some points. 'You can never approve of my having given up my situation while in Vienna.' I think, if I had been so disposed (which I really was not at the time, or I would have taken this step previously), it was the most judicious thing to do so in a place where I am liked, and have the finest prospects in the world. It is very possible that you could not sanction this in the presence of the Archbishop, but to me you cannot do otherwise than approve. 'I can in no other way redeem my honour than by retracting my resolution.' How could you write such a fallacy? It did not occur to you when you did so, that such a revocation would prove me to be the most dastardly man living. All Vienna knows that I have left the Archbishop, and also knows why – from my honour having been attacked, and for the third time too, and I am publicly to prove the contrary; thus making myself out a pitiful sneak, and the Archbishop a worthy Prince! The former no man would like to do, and least of all would I. The latter God alone can accomplish, if it be His will to enlighten him. 'I have never shown any love for you, and therefore ought to show it on this occasion.' Can you really say this? 'I have never sacrificed my own pleasures to yours.' What pleasures have I here? To be in trouble and anxiety to fill my purse. It seems to me that you really think I am revelling in pleasures and amusements. Oh! how completely are you mistaken – at all events, as matters now are! I have no more to spend than I absolutely require. The subscription for my six sonatas is going on, and then I shall get some money. It is all right, too, about the opera ['Die Entführung'], and in Advent I am to give a concert; after that, things will by degrees go on better, for a great deal is to be done here in winter. If pleasure means to have got away from a Prince who paid me badly and constantly bullied me, then it is true that my pleasure is great. If I were to do nothing but think and work from early dawn till night, I would gladly do so, rather than live on the favour of such a – but I will not trust myself to give him his right name. I was forced to take this step, and I will never deviate from it by a single hairsbreadth – impossible! All that I can say to you is how much I regret (for your sake – for yours alone, father) having been so badly treated; and I wish that the Archbishop had acted more judiciously, solely that I might have devoted my whole life to you. To please you, my kind father, I was prepared to sacrifice my health, my happiness, and my life; but honour is to me, and ought to be to you, beyond all else. You may show this to Count Arco, and to all Salzburg too. After such an insult – such a threefold insult – if the Archbishop *in propria persona* were to offer me 1,200 florins, I would not accept them. I am no low fellow, no rascal; and had it not been for your sake, I would not have waited for him to say to me the third time, 'Take yourself off,' without showing that I understood it to be final on both sides. What do I say – waited? I would have said it first myself instead of him. I am only surprised that the Archbishop should behave so indiscreetly in such a place as Vienna; but he shall one day see how entirely he was mistaken. Prince Breiner and Count Arco stand in need of the Archbishop, but I do not; and if it comes to the worst, and he forgets all the duties of a prince – a *spiritual* prince – then come to me at Vienna. You can get 400 florins anywhere. Only think how he would disgrace himself in the eyes of the Emperor, who already hates him, if he were to act thus. This place too would suit my sister far better than Salzburg; there are many distinguished families here who are reluctant to engage a male teacher, but would give handsome terms to a lady. This may all come to pass some day . . .

Mozart to his Father

Vienna, 9 June 1781

A pretty business Count Arco has now made of it! So this is the way to persuade me to follow his advice – to refuse to present a memorial through inborn stupidity – not to venture to say one word to his master from want of spirit and love of toadyism – to keep me in suspense for four weeks, and at last compel me to present the memorial myself, and instead of *at least* giving me free access to the Prince, to turn me out of doors with a kick! Such then is Count Arco, who (according to your last letter) has my interest so much at heart; such is the court I serve! When I arrive with a written document to present, instead of my wish being facilitated I am maltreated! The scene took place in the anteroom. Of course there was nothing to be done but to be gone with all speed, not wishing to show disrespect for the Prince's apartments, though Arco had not scrupled to do so. I have written three different memorials, and which I five times endeavoured to present, and each time they have been refused. I have carefully preserved them, and whoever wishes to read them may do so, to convince himself that they do not contain anything at all offensive. At last, on receiving back my memorial from Herr von Kleinmayrn in the evening (for this is his office), and the Archbishop's departure being fixed for the following day, I was perfectly frantic with rage;

I could not possibly allow him to set off thus, and as I was told by Arco (at least so he assured me) that the Prince knew nothing of it, I felt how angry the Archbishop would be with me for being so long here, and then at the last moment coming with such a document. I therefore wrote another, in which I mentioned that it was now five weeks since I had prepared a similar paper, but finding myself, why I did not know, always put off, I was now forced to present it myself, though at the very last moment. This memorial procured me my discharge in the pleasant way I have above described, and who knows whether it was not done by command of the Archbishop himself? Herr von Kleinmayrn, if he still wishes to maintain the character of an honest man, and also the Archbishop's servants, can testify that his commands were fulfilled. I need forward no petition; the thing is at an end. I shall write no more on the subject, and if the Archbishop were now to offer me 1,200 florins of salary I would never serve him again after such treatment. How easily I might have been persuaded to remain! – by kindness, but not by insolence and violence. I sent a message to Count Arco, that *I would have nothing to say to him*, because he spoke so harshly, behaving to me as if I had been a rogue, which he had no right to do; and, by heavens! as I already wrote to you, I never would have gone near him, if he had not sent me a message that he had a letter from you; but it is the last time. What is it to him if I wish to get my discharge? And if he had really been disposed to do me a good turn, he ought to have reasoned quietly with me, and allowed the affair to take its course, but not to bandy such words with me as clown and saucy fellow, and turn me out of the room with a kick; but I forget that this was probably by archiepiscopal command...

Mozart to his Father
Vienna, 16 June 1781

Tomorrow the portrait and the ribbons for my sister are to be despatched. I don't know whether the ribbons will suit her taste, but they are in the very last fashion. If she wishes to have some more, or perhaps some plain ones, she has only to let me know, and if there is anything else that she thinks may be got better in Vienna, she must write to me. I hope she did not pay for the cloth, as it is already paid for. I forgot to mention this, for I had so much to write about that scandalous affair. I will remit the money as you direct.

I can at length write you something about Vienna, for hitherto I have been obliged to fill my letters with that vile history; but it is now over, God be praised! This present season is, as you know, the worst for any one who wishes to make money. The most distinguished families are in the country, so all I can do at this moment is to work, to be in readiness for the winter, when there is less time to do so. As soon as the sonatas are finished,

I will look out for a short Italian cantata and write it, so that it may be given at the theatre during Advent, of course for my own benefit. There is a little cunning in this, for then I can give it twice, and with double profit, for when performed the second time I shall also perform on the piano. I have only one pupil at present – Countess Rumbeck, Cobenzl's cousin. I could indeed have had many more if I had chosen to lower my terms, but by doing so I should have injured my credit. My terms are six ducats for twelve lessons, and I also make it understood that I do even this from complaisance. I would rather have three pupils who pay me well than six who pay badly. *I can just get on* by means of this one pupil, and that is enough for the present. I mention this that you may not think me guilty of selfishness in sending you only thirty ducats. Believe me, I would gladly deprive myself of everything, if I only had it; but it is sure to come in time, and it is best never to let people know how one really stands.

About the theatre. I think I wrote to you lately that Count Rosenberg, before his departure, requested Schröder to hunt out a libretto for me. It is now come, and Stephanie [junior] has it in his hands as supervisor of the opera. Bergobzoomer, a true and kind friend both of mine and Schröder's, gave me an immediate hint of the fact. So I went to Stephanie at once, as if for a mere visit, for we thought it possible that his partiality for Umlauf [court musician] might induce him to play me false; this suspicion proved, however, quite unfounded, for I afterwards heard by chance that he had begged some one to ask me to call on him, as he wished to speak to me; and the moment I came in he said, 'Here you come in the very nick of time!' The opera is in four acts, and he tells me the first act is incomparable, but that it falls off very much. If Schröder will allow it to be altered as we think advisable, a good libretto may be made out of it. Stephanie does not like to give it to the directors as it now is, before having talked to Schröder on the subject, knowing beforehand that it would be rejected; so these two may settle the matter between them. After what Stephanie said, I did not express any desire to read it, for if it does not please me, I must say so plainly, or I should be the victim, and I do not wish to make Schröder unfriendly towards me, as he has great esteem for me at present; and as it is, I can always make the excuse that I have not read it.

I must explain why we were suspicious of Stephanie. I regret to say that he bears the worst reputation in Vienna, as a rude, false, calumnious person, not scrupling to commit the grossest injustice towards any one; but I don't mix myself up with such matters. There may be some truth in it, as he is found fault with by every one, but he is in great favour with the Emperor, and towards myself he was most friendly the very first time I saw him, saying, 'We are already old friends, and I shall be very glad if it be in my power to serve you in any way.' I believe and hope that he may write the libretto of an opera himself for me. Whether he wrote his own comedies, or did so with the aid of others, whether he plagiarised or originated, still he understands the stage, and his plays are invariably popular. I have lately seen two new pieces of his, which are certainly excellent, 'Das Loch in der Thüre' and 'Der Oberamtmann und die Soldaten'. In the meantime, I will compose the cantata, for even if I had a libretto, I would not put pen to paper, as Count Rosenberg is not here; and if at the last moment he did not approve of the book, I should have had the honour of writing for nothing, so I mean to steer clear of it at present. I don't care what the subject is, provided the libretto be only good. Do you really suppose that I am likely to write an *opera comique* in the same style as an *opera seria*? There should be as little sprightliness in an *opera seria*, and as much learning and solidity, as there should be little learning in an *opera buffa*, but all the more sprightliness and gaiety. That people like to have a little comic music in an *opera seria* I cannot help; but here they draw the proper distinction on this point. I do certainly find that in music the merry-andrew is not yet got rid of, and in this respect the French are right.

I hope to receive my clothes safely by the next diligence. I don't know when it goes, but I think this letter will reach you first, so I beg you will keep the cane to oblige me. Canes are used here, but why? – to walk with, and for that purpose any one will do. So pray lean on the cane instead of on me, and always take it with you when you can. Who knows whether it may not by your hand avenge its former master on Arco? – of course I mean accidentally, by mere chance! My *very practical* reply shall not fail that arrogant jackass, were it twenty years hence; for to see him and to return his kick without an instant's delay, will be one and the same thing, unless I am so unlucky as to see him first in some sacred place.

Mozart to his Father
Vienna, 8 August 1781

I must write quickly, for I have only this instant finished the Janissary chorus; it is past twelve o'clock, and I have promised to drive with the Aurnhammers and Cavalieri, at two o'clock precisely, to Mingendorf, near Luxemburg, where the camp is. Adamberger, Cavalieri, and Fischer are exceedingly pleased with their arias. I dined yesterday with Countess Thun, and am to do so again tomorrow. I played to her the portions I have completed, and at the end she said she would stake her life that what I have written so far cannot *fail to please.* In a point of this kind I *place no value on any man's praise or censure*, before people hear and see it as a whole, and I continue simply to follow my own feelings. You may, however, see from this how pleased people must be to speak in such a manner ...

Mozart to his Father
Vienna, 26 September 1781

The opera began with my monologue, so I asked Herr Stephanie to write an arietta for it, and then, after Osmin's little song, when the two talk together, to substitute a duett. We intend the part of Osmin for Herr Fischer, who certainly has a grand bass voice (although the Archbishop once assured me that he sang too low for a bass, and I in return promised that he should sing higher next time), so we must take advantage of this, especially as he has the whole public in his favour here. In the original libretto Osmin has only one song, and nothing else to sing except in the terzetto and finale; so now he has an aria in the first act, and also one in the second. I have already indicated to Stephanie the words that I require for that air, the chief part of the music being finished before Stephanie heard a word on the subject. There is only a beginning and an end, which must have a good effect, and Osmin's rage is made comical by the accompaniment of the Turkish music. In working out the aria, I have given full scope to Fischer's fine deep tones to vibrate. The 'D'rum beim Barte des Propheten' is indeed in the same time, but with quick notes, and as his wrath gradually increases (when the aria appears to be at an end), the *allegro assai* follows in quite another measure and key, which must insure the best effect; for as a man in such a violent fit of passion transgresses all the bounds of order and propriety, and forgets himself in his fury, the same must be the case with the music too. But as the passions, whether violent or not, must never be expressed so as to become revolting, and the music even in the most appalling situations never offend the ear, but continue to please and be melodious, I did not go from F, in which the air is written, into a remote key, but into an analogous one, not however into its nearest relative D minor, but into the more remote A minor. Do you know how I have expressed Belmonte's aria in A major, 'O wie ängstlich, o wie feurig', and the 'throbbing heart'? By octaves on the violins. This is the favourite aria of all those who have heard it, and mine also, and written expressly to suit Adamberger's voice. You hear the trembling, throbbing, swelling breast expressed by a crescendo; while the whispers and sighs are rendered by the first violins with *sordini*, and a flute in unison. The Janissary chorus is, as such, all that can be desired – short and lively, and written entirely to please the Viennese. I have rather sacrificed Constanze's aria to the flexible throat of Madlle. Cavalieri – 'Trennung war mein banges Loos' I have endeavoured to express so far as an Italian bravura air will admit of it. I have changed the *Hui* into *schnell*, so it now stands thus – 'Doch wie schnell schwand meine Freude!' I don't know what our German poets think; even if they do not understand the theatre, or at all events operas, still they should not make their personages talk as if they were addressing a herd of swine.

Now about the terzetto at the close of the first act. Pedrillo has passed off his master as an architect, to give him an opportunity to meet his Constanze in the garden. The Pacha has taken him into his service. Osmin the superintendent knows nothing of this, and being a rude churl and a sworn foe to all strangers, he is insolent, and refuses to let them enter the garden. This beginning is very short, and as the words admitted of it I wrote it very passably for the three voices; then comes the major at once *pianissimo*; it must go very quick, and wind up noisily at the close, which is always appropriate at the conclusion of an act; the more noise the better, the shorter the better, so that the people may not have time to cool in their applause. The overture is quite short with alternate *pianos* and *fortes*, the Turkish music always coming in at the *fortes*. It is modulated through different keys, and I think no one can well go to sleep over it, even if his previous night has been a sleepless one.

Now comes the rub! The first act has been ready for three weeks past, and likewise an aria in the second act, and the drunken duett, which in fact consists entirely of my Turkish tatoo, but I cannot go on with it just now, as the whole story is being altered, and by my own desire. At the beginning of the third act there is a charming quintett, or rather finale, but I should prefer having it at the end of the second act. In order to make this practicable, great changes must be made, and in fact an entirely new plot introduced; but Stephanie is already over head and ears in other work.

Mozart to his Father
Vienna, 13 October 1781

...Now as to the libretto of the opera. So far as regards Stephanie's work you are quite right; still the poetry is strictly in keeping with the character of the stupid, surly, malicious Osmin. I am well aware that this species of verse is not the best, but it chimed in so admirably with my musical ideas (previously rambling about in my head) that it could not fail to please me, and I would lay a wager that when it is performed no deficiencies will be found. As for the poetry in the piece itself, I really do not consider it at all despicable. The aria of Belmonte, 'O wie ängstlich!' could not possibly be better written for the music. The 'Hui' and 'Kummer ruht in meinem Schoosz' excepted (as grief and repose are incompatible), the air is not badly written, particularly the first part, and I should say that in an opera the poetry must necessarily be the obedient daughter of the music. Why do the Italian comic operas everywhere please – with all their wretched poetry – even in Paris, where I myself witnessed the fact? Because music rules there supreme, and all else is forgotten. An opera is certain to become popular when the plot is well worked out, the verse written expressly for the music, and not merely to suit some miserable rhyme (which never enhances the value of any theatrical performance, be it what it may, but rather detracts from it), bringing in words or even entire verses, which completely ruin the whole ideas of the composer. Versification is, indeed, indispensable for music, but rhyme, solely for rhyming's sake, most pernicious. Those gentlemen who set to work in this pedantic fashion will always insure the failure both of their book and of the music. It would be well if a good composer could be found who understood the stage, with talent enough to make suggestions, and combined with that true Phœnix – an intellectual poet; then no misgivings would be entertained about the applause even of the unlearned. Poets seem to me somewhat like trumpeters with their mechanical tricks! If we musical composers were to adhere as faithfully to our rules (which were very good at a time when no one knew any better), we should compose music as worthless as their libretti. But I think I have given you a pretty long digression, so I must now enquire about what I have always most at heart – your health, dearest father. I proposed in my last letter two remedies for your vertigo, which, if you do not know them, you may not value, but I have been assured that they are certain to have a good effect; and the pleasure of thinking you might get quite well, made me so entirely believe this assurance, that I could not resist naming them to you at once. My most sincere wish is that you may not require them; but, on the other hand, they might contribute to your entire recovery. I trust my sister is now daily improving in health.

Work on Die Entführung *continued to be held up, and the opera was not eventually performed until the following summer. But Mozart was beginning to make his way in Vienna, and a much-publicized keyboard contest with the Italian piano virtuoso Muzio Clementi, before the Emperor and a group of distinguished guests, helped to establish his name. Meanwhile, his last tussle with his father was over his marriage. Mozart's involvement with the Weber family (first cousins of the composer of* Der Freischütz*) went back to his first visit to Mannheim in 1778, when it had been the second daughter, Aloisia Weber, who had taken his fancy. But by now Aloisia was married to the actor, Joseph Lange, and Mozart, who had taken a room in the Webers' Viennese apartment at the time of his break with the Archbishop, fell in love with the third daughter, Constanze. He was obviously not sure of the reception which this development would receive from his father.*

Mozart to his Father

Vienna, 15 December 1781

...My very dearest father, you demand an explanation of the words in the closing sentence of my last letter. Oh! how gladly would I long ago have opened my heart to you, but I was deterred by the reproaches I dreaded for even thinking of such a thing at so unseasonable a time, although merely *thinking* can never be unseasonable. My endeavours are directed at present to securing a small but certain income, which, together with what chance may put in my way, may enable me to live and – to marry! You are alarmed at this idea; but I entreat you, my dearest, kindest father, to listen to me. I have been obliged to disclose to you my purpose; you must therefore allow me to disclose to you my reasons also, and very well grounded reasons they are. My feelings are strong, but I cannot live as many other young men do. In the first place, I have too great a sense of religion, too much love for my neighbour to do so, and too high a feeling of honour to deceive any innocent girl. My disposition has always inclined me more to domestic life than to excitement; I never from my youth upwards have been in the habit of taking any charge of my linen or clothes, &c., and I think nothing is more desirable for me than a wife. I assure you I am forced to spend a good deal owing to the want of proper care of what I possess. I am quite convinced that I should be far better off with a wife (and the same income I now have), for how many other superfluous expenses would it save! Others come, to be sure, in their place, but I know what they are, and can regulate accordingly, and, in short, lead an orderly life. An unmarried man, in my opinion, enjoys only half a life. Such are my views, and such they will always remain. I have thought and reflected sufficiently, and I shall ever continue to think the same. But now who is the object of my love? Do not be startled, I entreat. Not one of the Webers, surely? Yes, one of the Webers — not Josepha, not Sophie, but the third daughter, Constanze. I never met with such diversity of dispositions in any family. The eldest is idle, coarse, and deceitful — crafty and cunning as a fox; Madame Lange [Aloysia] is false and unprincipled, and a coquette; the youngest is still too childish to have her character defined — she is merely a good-humoured, frivolous girl; may God guard her from temptation! The third, however, namely, my good and beloved Constanze, is the martyr of the family, and probably on this very account the kindest-hearted, the cleverest, and, in short, the best of them all; she takes charge of the whole house, and yet does nothing right in their eyes. Oh! my dear father, I could write you pages were I to describe to you all the scenes that I have witnessed in that house; but if you wish it I will do so in my next letter. Before, however, releasing you from this subject, I must make you better acquainted with the character of my Constanze. She is not plain, but at the same time far from being handsome; her whole beauty consists in a pair of bright black eyes and a pretty figure. She is not witty, but has enough sound good sense to enable her to fulfil her duties as a wife and mother. It is utterly false that she is inclined to be extravagant; on the contrary, she is invariably very plainly dressed, for the little her mother can spend on her children she gives to the two others, but to Constanze nothing. It is true that her dress is always neat and nice, however simple, and she can herself make most of the things requisite for a young lady. She dresses her own hair, understands housekeeping, and has the best heart in the world. I love her with my whole soul, as she does me. Tell me if I could wish for a better wife. I must add that, at the time I gave up my situation, my love had not begun; it first arose (while living with them) from her tender care and attentions. All I now wish is that I may procure some permanent situation (and this, thank God, I have good hopes of), and then I shall never cease entreating your consent to my rescuing this poor girl, and thus making, I may say, all of us quite happy, as well as Constanze and myself; for, if I am happy, you are sure to be so, dearest father, and one half of the proceeds of my situation shall be yours.

I have thus opened my heart to you, and fully explained my words. I in turn beg you to explain those in your last letter: 'You do not believe that I was aware of a proposal made to you, but to which you have given no answer?' I don't understand one word of this. I know of no proposal. Pray, have compassion on your son. Ever your dutiful son.

Mozart to his Father
Vienna, 22 December 1781

I am still full of wrath and indignation at the shameless lies of that arch-villain Winter. At the same time I feel calm and composed, because they do not affect me, and I am pleased and satisfied with you, my dearest and kindest of fathers. I never could expect anything else, however, from your good sense, and your kindness and love towards me. You have no doubt by this time received my last letter with the confession of my love and my intentions, and you will see by it that I am not such a fool as at the age of five-and-twenty to marry rashly without possessing any certain income. My reasons for wishing to marry soon are well grounded, and the picture I have drawn of my dear Constanze must show you how well fitted she is to become my wife, for she is just as I have described her, neither an atom better nor worse. As for the contract of marriage, I will make the most candid confession about it, thoroughly persuaded that you will forgive me this step, for had you been in my place you would most assuredly have done the same. For one thing alone I entreat your pardon – that is, for not having long ago written to you on the subject. In my last letter I apologised for the delay, and told you the cause that deterred me from writing. I do hope you will grant me your forgiveness, especially as no one was made more miserable by it than myself. Indeed, if you had not by your last letter given me an inducement to enter on the subject, I intended to have written to you and confessed everything; for no longer, no longer, by heavens! could I bear it.

But now in reference to the marriage contract, or rather to the written pledge of my honourable intentions with regard to the girl. You are well aware that her father being no longer alive (unhappily for the whole family as well as for Constanze and myself), a guardian stands in his place. To him (who is not acquainted with me) busybodies and officious gentlemen like Winter and others, must have no doubt brought all sorts of reports, such as, that he must beware of me, that I had no fixed income, that I frequented her society too much, that I would perhaps leave her in the lurch, and thus make the girl miserable, &c., &c. The guardian became very uneasy at these insinuations. The mother, however, who knows me and my integrity, was perfectly satisfied, and never said a word to him. My whole intercourse consisted in living in the same house with her, and afterwards calling every day. No one ever saw me with her elsewhere. The guardian besieged the mother with his remonstrances till she told me of them, and begged me to speak to him myself, as he was to be there shortly.

He came, and we conversed together, and the result was (as I did not explain myself so clearly as he desired) that he insisted on the mother putting an end to all intercourse between her daughter and myself until I had settled the affair with him in writing. The mother said, 'His whole intercourse consists in his calling here; I cannot forbid him my house; he is too good a friend of ours, and one to whom I am under great obligations. I am satisfied; I trust him. Settle it with him yourself.' So he forbade my seeing her at all, unless I gave him a written engagement. What could I do? I was forced either to give a contract in writing or renounce the girl. Who that sincerely and truly loves can forsake his beloved? Would not the mother of the girl herself have placed the worst interpretation on such conduct? Such was my position. The contract was in this form: – 'I bind myself to marry Madlle. Constanze Weber in the course of three years, and if it should so happen, which I consider impossible, that I change my mind, she shall be entitled to draw on me every year for 300 florins.' Nothing in the world could be easier than to write this, for I knew that the payment of the 300 florins never would be exacted, because I could never forsake her; and if unhappily I altered my views, I would only be too glad to get rid of her by paying the 300 florins; and Constanze, as I know her, would be too proud to let herself be sold in this way. But what did the angelic girl do when her guardian was gone? She desired her mother to give her the written paper, and saying to me 'Dear Mozart, I require no written contract from you, I rely on your promise,' she tore up the paper. This trait endeared Constanze still more to me, and by the destruction of the contract, and the faithful promise of the guardian to keep the affair secret, I was in so far at ease about you, dearest father. I was not uneasy about your consent to my marriage when the proper time arrived (as the girl has everything but money), for I know your rational ideas on these subjects. Will you then forgive me? I hope so. I do not doubt it.

I must now (however repugnant to me) speak of those vile slanderers. I believe Herr Reiner's sole malady must have consisted in having gone wrong in the head. I saw him by chance in the theatre, where he gave me a letter from Ramm [formerly hautboy-player in Mannheim, and now in Munich]. I asked him where he lodged, but he could neither tell me the street nor the house, and grumbled at having been over-persuaded to come here. I offered to present him to the Countess and wherever I had the *entrée*, and told him that if he found he could not give a concert, I would present him to the Grand-Duke. He said, 'Pooh! nothing is to be done here; I shall go away at once.' 'Only have a little patience,' said I; 'as you can't tell me where your lodging is, I shall at all events tell you mine, which is easily found.' He never came to see me; I enquired where to find him, but when I at last discovered his address, he was gone. So much for this gentleman! As for Winter, I can with truth say that on account of Vogler he has always been my greatest enemy. In his manners he resembles the brutes, and in the rest of his conduct and actions he is a mere child; so I really feel ashamed to write a single word about him, for he thoroughly deserves the contempt of every man of honour. I shall not, therefore, tell infamous truths of him in return for the infamous lies he told about me, but rather give you an account of my general mode of life.

Every morning at six o'clock comes my hairdresser and wakes me. I have finished dressing by seven, when I write till ten; I then give a lesson to Frau von Trattner. At eleven I go to Countess Rumbeck; each of these pupils gives me six ducats for twelve lessons, and I go there every day, unless they send to put me off, which always annoys me. I have settled with the Countess that she is never to put me off – that is, if she cannot receive me, I am to count the lesson all the same – but Frau von Trattner is too economical to do so. I don't owe any man a farthing. I never heard a word of any amateur concert where two persons played the piano beautifully, and I must frankly say that I do not think it worth while to answer all the trash repeated by such a miserable blockhead and gossip. If you can believe that I am hated at court and by all the nobility, or any part of them, you have only to write to Herr von Strack, Countess Thun, Countess Rumbeck, Baroness Waldstädten, Herr von

Sonnenfels, Frau von Trattner – in short, to whom you choose. For the present I shall only say that recently during dinner the Emperor praised me to the highest degree, adding these words, *'c'est un talent décidé'*; and the day before yesterday, the 14th, I played at court. Another pianist has arrived here, an Italian whose name is Clementi, and he was also engaged to play. I received fifty ducats yesterday for this, which I at present stand greatly in need of. My dear kind father, you will see that things now daily go better with me. What avails a great excitement? Sudden success is never lasting – *chi va piano va sano*. Let each cut his coat according to his cloth. Among all the shameful calumnies of Winter, the only thing that enrages me is that he disparages my Constanze! I have described her to you as she really is, and if you wish to know the opinion of others write to Herr von Aurnhammer, where she occasionally visits; she once dined there. Write to Baroness Waldstädten, with whom she was (unluckily) only one month, the Baroness being ill, and now her mother refuses to part with her. God grant I may soon be able to marry her! Cecarelli sends you his regards; he sang at court yesterday. Adieu!

Mozart to his Sister

Vienna, 20 April 1782

My dearest Sister,

My darling Constanze has at last summoned up courage to follow the impulse of her kind heart, and to write to you. If you are so good, dear sister, as to answer her (which I hope you will, that I may see the joy in this dear creature's face), I beg you will enclose your letter to me. I mention this as a precaution, to warn you that her mother and sisters are not aware that she has written to you. I enclose a prelude and a three-part fugue [Köchel, No. 394]. The reason that I did not write to you before was not being able to finish the music sooner, owing to the great trouble of writing out such small notes. It is awkwardly done, for the prelude ought to come first and the fugue to follow – the cause being that I composed the fugue first, and while writing it out I devised the prelude. I only hope you may be able to read it, as it is written so very small, but above all that it may please you. Another time I will send you something better for the piano. My dear Constanze is, in fact, the origin of this fugue coming into the world. Baron von Swieten, to whom I go every Sunday, gives me all Handel's and Sebastian Bach's fugues (after I have played them to him) to take home with me. When Constanze heard these, she fell in love with them at once; she will listen to nothing but fugues, and particularly the works (in this style) of Handel and Bach. As she had often heard me play fugues out of my head, she asked me if I never wrote them down; and when I said I never did, she reproached me for not having composed this most artistic and beautiful style of music, and never ceased her entreaties till I wrote a fugue for her. So this is its origin. I have purposely timed it *andante maestoso*, that it may not be played too quick; for if a fugue is not rather slowly played, the subject as it comes in cannot be distinctly and clearly heard, and thus naturally produces no effect. In the course of time, and when I have a favourable opportunity, I intend to write five others, and present them to Baron von Swieten, whose collection of music, though small in numbers, is great in value. So on this account I beg you to adhere to your promise not to show it to a soul. Learn it by heart and play it. A fugue is not easily caught by another person from merely hearing it. If papa has not yet had Eberlin's works transcribed, so much the better, for I got them from a friend (as I could not quite remember them), and now, unhappily, I see that they are too trivial to deserve a place beside Handel and Bach. I would speak with all due respect of his four-part writings, but his pianoforte fugues are nothing but interludes drawn out to a great length. Goodbye! I am glad you find the two caps suit you.

Mozart to Constanze Weber

Vienna, 29 April 1782

My dear and beloved Friend,

Ýou still, I hope, allow me to give you this name?
Surely you do not hate me so much that I may no longer
be your friend, nor you mine? And even if you do not
choose henceforth to be called my friend, you cannot
prevent my thinking of you as tenderly as I have always
done. Reflect well on what you said to me today. In
spite of all my entreaties, you have met me on three
occasions with a flat refusal, and told me plainly that
you wished to have no more to do with me. It is not,
however, a matter of the same indifference to me that it
seems to be to you, to lose the object of my love; I am
not, therefore, so passionate, so rash, or so reckless, as
to accept your refusal. I love you too dearly for such a
step. I beg you then once more to weigh well and calmly
the cause of our quarrel, which arose from my being
displeased at your telling your sisters (N.B., in my
presence) that at a game of forfeits you had allowed the
size of your leg to be measured by a gentleman.)* No
girl with becoming modesty would have permitted such

---

* A fine at a game of forfeits, which testifies the freedom and levity of
the society of that day, and must be measured according to the social
tone and usages of that time rather than with those of propriety. The
reputation of Baroness Waldstädten, who, it appears, had done the
same, did not stand very high.

a thing. The maxim to do as others do is well enough, but there are many things to be considered besides – whether only intimate friends and acquaintances are present – whether you are a child, or a girl old enough to be married – more especially whether you are already betrothed – but, above all, whether you are with people of much higher rank than yourself. If it be true that the Baroness [Waldstädten] did the same, still it is quite another thing, because she is a *passée* elderly woman (who cannot possibly any longer charm), and is always rather flighty. I hope, my dear friend, that you will never lead a life like hers, even should you resolve never to become my wife. But the thing is past, and a candid avowal of your heedless conduct would have made me at once overlook it, and allow me to say, if you will not be offended, my dearest friend, will still make me do so. This will show you how truly I love you. *I do not fly into a passion like you.* I think, I reflect, and I feel. *If you feel, and have feeling*, then I know I shall be able this very day to say with a tranquil mind: My Constanze is the virtuous, honourable, discreet, and faithful darling of her honest and kindly-disposed Mozart.

Mozart to his Father
Vienna, 20 July 1782

I hope you safely received my last letter, in which I gave you an account of the good reception of my opera. It was given yesterday for the second time, when perhaps you will scarcely believe that there was even a stronger cabal against it than on the first evening. The whole of the first act was scrambled through, which, however, could not prevent the loud shouts of bravo during the airs. My hopes rested on the closing terzett, but my evil star permitted Fischer to go wrong, which made Dauer (Pedrillo) go wrong also; and Adamberger alone could not sustain the whole, so that all the effect was lost, and this time it was *not encored*. I was in such a rage (and so was Adamberger) that my blood boiled, and I said that I never again would allow the opera to be given without a previous rehearsal for the singers. In the second act both the duetts were encored the same as the first night, and also Belmonte's rondo, 'Wenn der Freude Thränen fliessen'. The theatre was almost more crowded than on the previous evening. Not a stall was to be had the day before, either in the pit or in the third gallery, nor a box of any kind. The opera has brought 1,200 florins in the two days. I send you herewith the original and two of the little books, in which you will find a great many erasures, knowing that the score would be instantly copied out here; I therefore gave free course to my thoughts, and before allowing it to be transcribed, I first marked the different alterations and curtailments, and it was performed just as you now have it. I have missed out here and there the trumpets and kettle-drums, the flutes, clarionets, and Turkish music, because I could not get any music-paper with a sufficient number of lines, so they are written on extra paper, which the copyist has no doubt lost; at all events, he could not find them. The first act (when I was taking it to some one, I forget who), unluckily fell into the mud, which causes it to be so dirty.

I have now no little trouble in arranging my opera for a band by Sunday week, or some one will anticipate me and secure the profits instead of me; and yet you propose to me to compose a new symphony.* How is such a thing possible? You have no idea of the difficulty of arranging a work of this kind for a band – to adapt it to the wind instruments, yet without detracting from the effect. Well, all I can do is to devote the night to the task, for it cannot be managed otherwise, and to you, dear father, I sacrifice it. You may rely on having something from me by every post, and I will write it as quickly as I can and as well as haste will permit.

Count Zichi has this moment sent to me to say that he wishes me to drive with him to Saxenburg, that he may present me to Prince Kaunitz. I must therefore conclude, as I have yet to dress, for, when I have no intention of going out, I always remain *en négligé*. The copyist has this moment sent me the other parts. Adieu! – P.S. My dear Constanze's love to both.

---

* The father had begged him to send a symphony in honour of a family festival at Hafner's house in Salzburg.

Mozart to his Father
Vienna, 27 July 1782

... My dear kind father, I do implore you, by all you
hold dear in the world, to give me your consent to my
marrying my beloved Constanze. Do not suppose that
it is marriage alone I think of – in that case I would
gladly submit to wait – but I see that it is absolutely
necessary for my own honour and also that of my
Constanze, as well as for my health and peace of mind;
my heart is troubled, my head confused; in such a state
how is it possible either to think or to work to any good
purpose? And whence does this arise? Most people
think we are already married, which irritates the
mother, and the poor girl (as well as myself) is tor-
mented to death. This can easily be obviated. Believe
me it is as practicable to live in expensive Vienna as
anywhere else; everything depends upon proper housekeeping and management, which never can be expected
from a young man, especially when in love. The man
who gets such a wife as I shall may well be happy. We
intend to live in a most private and retired manner. Do
not be uneasy. If I were this very day to be taken ill,
which may God forbid! I may venture to assert that
(especially if married) the very highest of the nobility
here would take me under their protection. I can say
this with entire confidence. I know the way in which
Prince Kaunitz spoke of me to the Emperor, and to the

Archduke Maximilian. I shall anxiously expect your consent, my kind father. I feel sure that I shall receive it, for my honour and my reputation are at stake. Do not too long defer the pleasure of welcoming your son and his wife.

P.S. – I embrace my dear sister. Constanze's love to you both.

Mozart to the Baroness von Waldstädten

Vienna, shortly before 4 August 1782

Highly esteemed Lady,

I received my music by a maidservant of Madame Weber's, and was obliged to give a written receipt for it. The maid confided to me something which I can scarcely believe, as it would entail such disgrace on the family; yet as, to those who know the folly of Madame Weber, nothing seems impossible, I feel very uneasy. Sophie came out in tears, and when the maid asked her what was the matter, she said: 'Tell Mozart privately to manage to send Constanze home; otherwise my mother is quite determined to make the police fetch her.' Have the police really the power to enter any house they please? Perhaps this may only be a snare to lure her home. But if it could be so, our only resource is that Constanze should marry me early tomorrow, or this very day, if possible; for I will not expose my darling to such an insult, from which as my wife she is secure.

Another thing. Herr von Thorwarth is to be at the Webers' today. Pray give me your kind advice, and lend a helping hand to us poor creatures. I shall wait all day at home. In the greatest haste. Constanze knows nothing as yet of this. Did Herr von Thorwarth call on you? Is it necessary that we should both go to see him after dinner today?

Mozart to his Father
Vienna, 7 August 1782

You are very much mistaken in your son if you can believe him capable of base conduct. My beloved Constanze, now, thank God, at last my wife, knew my circumstances long ago, and heard from me that I had nothing whatever to expect from you;* but her attachment and love for me were so great, that she gladly and joyfully sacrificed her future life to share my fate. I thank you, with all the tender affection a son must always feel towards a father, for your kind consent and blessing. I felt I could rely on it; and you knew that I was myself only too well aware of all – all that could be said against such a step; but without injury to my conscience

---

* The father, when he at last gave his consent to the marriage, desired Wolfgang to observe that he (the father) could no longer expect assistance from his son in his distressed circumstances, caused by his efforts to promote that son's welfare; that Wolfgang, in return, must not hope, either now or hereafter, to receive anything from his father, and that he wished his bride to be told this.

and my honour I could not act otherwise, and I knew I could place implicit confidence in your consent. After waiting two posts in vain for your answer, the day of our wedding having been finally settled (by which time your reply ought to have arrived), being quite assured of your consent, I was married, by the blessing of God, to my beloved Constanze. Next day I received both your letters at once. Now the event has taken place, and I entreat your forgiveness for my perhaps too hasty trust in your fatherly love. This candid confession gives you a fresh proof of my regard for truth, and my detestation of falsehood. My dear wife will herself by the next post write to her kind father-in-law to entreat his blessing, and to her beloved sister-in-law to solicit the continuance of her valued friendship. No one attended the marriage but Constanze's mother and youngest sister, Herr von Thorwarth in his capacity of guardian, Herr von Zetto (Landrath) who gave away the bride, and Gilofsky [of Salzburg] as my best man. When the ceremony was over, both my wife and I shed tears; all present (even the priest) were touched on seeing the emotion of our hearts. Our sole wedding festivities consisted of a supper, which Baroness Waldstädten gave us, and indeed it was more princely than baronial. My darling is now a hundred times more joyful at the idea of going to Salzburg; and I am willing to stake – ay, my very life, that you will rejoice still more in my happiness when you really know her; if, indeed, in your estimation, as in mine, a high-principled, honest, virtuous, and pleasing wife ought to make a man happy.

I send you herewith a short march. I hope that all will arrive in due time, and be to your taste. The first *allegro* must be played with much fire, the last as *prestissimo* as possible. My opera (by Gluck's desire) was given again yesterday. Gluck was very complimentary to me about it. I dine with him tomorrow. You see in what haste I write. My dear wife and I kiss your hands a thousand times.

Mozart to the Baroness von Waldstädten
Vienna, 15 February 1783

Highly esteemed Lady,*

I am now in a fine dilemma! Herr von Tranner and I lately agreed to ask for a renewal of our bill for fourteen days. As every merchant does this kind of thing, unless he is the most disobliging man in the world, I was quite at ease, hoping by that time to have been able to borrow the sum if I could not manage to pay it myself, and now Herr von Tranner today sends to let me know that the person in question absolutely refuses to wait, and that if I do not pay the money before tomorrow he

---

* It appears by the marriage contract that the wedding portion was 500 florins, and the settlement 1,000 florins. The Baroness Waldstädten seems to have been of no small use in procuring this sum.

will *sue me at law.* Only think, dear lady, what a distressing occurrence this would be for me! I have no means of paying the money at present, nor even so much as one half. If I could have had the least idea that the subscriptions for my concert would proceed so slowly, I would have got the money at a longer date. I do entreat you, honoured lady, for heaven's sake to assist in preserving my reputation and my good name. My poor little wife is so unwell that I cannot leave her, or I would have gone to you myself to entreat your good offices in person. We kiss your hands 1,000 times, and remain your dutiful children,

W. A. and C. Mozart

Mozart to his Father
Vienna, 7 June 1783

... I must here say a few words to my sister about the Clementi sonatas. Every one who either hears them or plays them, must feel that as compositions they are poor enough. They contain no remarkable or striking passages, except those in sixths and octaves, and I beg my sister not to practise these *too much*, that she may not disturb her quiet even touch, nor injure the natural lightness, facility, and smooth rapidity of her finger. For, after all, what is to be gained by it? Supposing that you do play the sixths and octaves with the utmost velocity (which no man, not even Clementi, can thoroughly accomplish), you produce an unpleasant scramble, but nothing else in the world. Clementi is a *charlatan*, like *all Italians*. He writes *presto* over a sonata, and often *prestissimo* and *alla breve*, and plays it himself *allegro* in $\frac{4}{4}$ time. I know this to be the case, for I heard him do so. What he really does well are his passages in thirds, but he laboured at these day and night in London. Except these he can do nothing, absolutely nothing, for he has not the slightest taste or execution, far less feeling.

Between 1782 and the beginning of 1785 Mozart gradually became more and more in demand as performer, teacher and composer: this was the period of the 'Haffner' and 'Linz' Symphonies, the first nine of the mature Piano Concertos written for his own Viennese performances, and the first of the great String Quartets later dedicated to Haydn. Nevertheless he was continually short of money, and from this period onward letters to various friends asking for financial help become a recurrent feature of his correspondence. But this was not the aspect of his son's life which Leopold Mozart saw when he paid a last visit to Vienna early in 1785.

Leopold Mozart to his Daughter
Vienna, 16 February 1785

... We arrived at the Schulerstrasse No. 846, first floor, at one o'clock on Friday. That your brother has very fine quarters with all the necessary furniture you may gather from the fact that his rent is 460 gulden. On the same evening we drove to his first subscription concert, at which a great many members of the aristocracy were present. Each person pays a souverain d'or or three ducats for these Lenten concerts. Your brother is giving them at the Mehlgrube and only pays half a souverain d'or each time for the hall. The concert was magnificent and the orchestra played superbly. In addition to the symphonies a female singer of the Italian theatre sang two arias. Then we had a new and very fine concerto [K466] by Wolfgang, which the copyist was still copying when we arrived, and the rondo of which your brother did not even have time to play through, as he had to supervise the copying. You can well imagine that I met many old acquaintances there who all came up to speak to me. I was also introduced to several other people.

On Saturday evening Herr Joseph Haydn and the two Barons Tinti came to see us and the new quartets were performed, or rather, the three new ones [K458, 464 and 465] which Wolfgang has added to the other three which we have already. The new ones are somewhat easier, but at the same time excellent compositions. Haydn said to me: 'Before God and as an honest man I tell you that your son is the greatest composer known to me either in person or by name. He has taste and, what is more, the most profound knowledge of composition.'

On Sunday evening the Italian singer, Madame Laschi, who is leaving for Italy, gave a concert in the theatre, at which she sang two arias. A cello concerto was performed, a tenor and a bass each sang an aria and your brother played a glorious concerto, which he composed for Mlle Paradis for Paris. I was sitting only two boxes away from the very beautiful Princess of Wurtemberg and had the great pleasure of hearing so clearly all the interplay of the instruments that for sheer delight tears came into my eyes. When your brother left the platform the Emperor waved his hat and called out 'Bravo, Mozart!' And when he came on to play, there was a great deal of clapping.

We were not at the theatre yesterday, for every day there is a concert. This evening there is another one in the theatre, at which your brother is again playing a concerto. I shall bring back several of his new compositions. Little Carl is the picture of him. He seems very healthy, but now and then, of course, children have trouble with their teeth. On the whole the child is charming, for he is extremely friendly and laughs when spoken to. I have only seen him cry once and the next moment he started to laugh . . .

Mozart to Joseph Haydn*

Vienna, 1 September 1785

To my dear friend Haydn,

A father having resolved to send forth his children into the wide world, is anxious to confide them to the protection and guidance of a man who enjoys much celebrity there, and who fortunately is moreover his best friend. Here then are the children I intrust to a man so renowned, and so dear to me as a friend. These are, it is true, the fruits of a long and laborious study, but my hopes, grounded on experience, lead me to anticipate that my labours may, at least in some degree, be compensated; and they will, I flatter myself; one day prove a source of consolation to me. During your last stay in this capital, you yourself, my dearest friend, expressed your satisfaction with regard to them. This suffrage from you above all inspires me with the wish to offer them to you, and leads me to hope that they will not seem to you wholly unworthy of your favour. Be pleased then to receive them kindly, and be to them a father, a guide, and a friend. From this moment I transfer to you all my rights over them; but I entreat you to look with indulgence on those defects which may have escaped the too partial eye of a father, and, in spite

* A dedication, in Italian, published in Arataria's first edition of the six string quartets K387, 421, 428, 458, 464 and 465, which Mozart had composed during the years 1782 to 1785.

of these, to continue your generous friendship towards one who so highly appreciates it; and in the meantime I am from my heart your sincere friend,

Mozart

Mozart to Franz Anton Hoffmeister
Vienna, 20 November 1785

Dear Hoffmeister,

I have recourse to you to beg that you will advance me some money, of which I stand in great need at this moment. I beg further that you will be so good as to try to obtain the money for me as soon as possible. Forgive my importunity, but as you know me, and are well aware how anxious I am that what I write for you should be good, I feel convinced that you will pardon me for plaguing you, and that you will gladly be of as much service to me as I wish to be to you.

By the beginning of 1787 Mozart had embarked on his last great creative period. The success of Le nozze di Figaro *in Vienna eight months earlier had just been repeated in Prague, and a new opera (*Don Giovanni*) commissioned for the following season in the Bohemian capital. The last symphonies, concertos and chamber works,* Cosí fan tutte, Die Zauberflöte, La clemenza di Tito *and the Requiem were still to come. But his father's death put an end to the flood of* *correspondence between the two men which gives so lively a picture of Mozart's working life in earlier years, and during his last four years his letters are mainly concerned with his financial difficulties, asking for one loan after another from his Freemason friends (he had become a Mason himself in 1784), or to his wife in Baden where she went to take cures in each of the three years before his death.*

Mozart to Baron Gottfried von Jacquin, Vienna
Prague, 15 January 1787

My dearest Friend,

At last I find a moment to write to you. Soon after my arrival I intended to have written four letters to Vienna, but in vain! – one only (to my mother-in-law) I did contrive partly to accomplish, for I could only write one half, and my wife and Hofer [the husband of his sister-in-law Josepha] were obliged to finish it for me. The moment we arrived (Thursday, the 11th, at twelve o'clock in the forenoon) we had hard work to get ready for dinner, which was at one o'clock. After dinner, old Count Thun entertained us with some music, executed by his own people, which lasted about an hour and a half. This is a *real amusement*, and one which I can enjoy every day. At six o'clock I went with Count Canal to what is called the Breitfeld Ball, where the flower of the Prague beauties assemble. You ought to have been there, my dear friend; I think I see you running, or rather limping, after all those pretty creatures, married and single. I neither danced nor flirted with any of them, the former because I was too tired, and the latter from my natural bashfulness. I saw, however, with the greatest pleasure, all these people flying about with such delight to the music of my 'Figaro', transformed into quadrilles and waltzes; for here nothing is talked of but 'Figaro', nothing played but 'Figaro', nothing whistled or sung but 'Figaro', no opera so crowded as 'Figaro', nothing but 'Figaro' – very flattering to me, certainly. As I came home very late from the ball, and very tired and sleepy from my journey besides, nothing could be more natural than my sleeping very late next day, which was just what I did; so the whole of the next morning was again *sine linea*. After dinner the Count's music was to be listened to, and as on the same day I got an excellent piano in my room, you may easily imagine that I could not leave it untouched for a whole evening; so I played, and, as a matter of course, we performed a little *Quatuor in caritatis camera* ('*und das schöne Bandl hammera*',* and in this way the whole evening was likely to pass again *sine linea*, and so it actually did. You must chide Morpheus, not me – a deity who is only too kind to us in Prague. What the cause may be I know not, but at any rate we both went to sleep very quickly. Still we managed to be at Father Unger's by eleven o'clock,

---

* A comic trio of Mozart's. Köchel, No. 441.

and to make a thorough inspection of the Imperial Library and the public Theological Seminary. After we had almost stared our eyes out of our heads, we listened to a little remonstrance from within, so we considered it advisable to drive to Count Canal's to dinner. The evening surprised us sooner than you could believe, when it was time to go to the opera. We heard '*Le Gare generose*' [of Paesiello]. I can give no positive opinion about the performance of this opera, because I talked so much; perhaps the reason of my being so loquacious, quite contrary to my usual custom, might be well, never mind! the evening was, *al solito*, frittered away. Today I have at last been so fortunate as to find a moment to enquire after the health of your excellent parents, and all the Jacquin family. I hope and trust you may all be as well as we are. I must candidly confess (though I meet with all possible politeness and courtesy here, and Prague is indeed a very beautiful and agreeable place), that I very much long to return to Vienna, and I do assure you the chief cause of this is certainly *your family.* When I think that after my return I shall only have so short an enjoyment of your valued society, and then be so long, perhaps indeed for ever, deprived of this happiness, I thoroughly feel the extent of the friendship and esteem I cherish for your whole family.

And now, my dearest friend, adieu! My concert is to take place in the theatre next Friday, the 19th, which will, alas! prolong my stay here. I send my kind regards to your worthy parents, and best wishes to your brother [Joseph, his father's successor]. I beg also a thousand compliments to your sister [Franziska, one of Mozart's best scholars]; tell her I hope she will practise very assiduously on her new piano, though such an admonition is unnecessary, for I must say that I never had so industrious a pupil, or one who showed so much zeal as herself, and indeed I quite rejoice at the thoughts of giving her further instructions, according to my ability.

I suppose it is high time now to conclude – is it not? You probably have thought so some time since. Farewell, my dear friend! I hope you will always feel the same friendship for me. Write to me soon – really *soon*; or if you are too idle to do so yourself, send for Salzmann and dictate a letter to him, though no letter seems to come really from the heart unless written by your own hand. Well, I shall see whether you are as truly my friend as I am, and ever shall be, yours,

Mozart

P.S. – Address the letter you may *possibly* write to me, 'im Graf Thunischen Palais'. My wife sends her love to all the Jacquin family, and also to Herr Hofer. On Wednesday next I am to see and hear 'Figaro', unless I become blind and deaf before then. Perhaps I may not become so till *after* the opera!

Mozart to his Father

Vienna, 4 April 1787

Mon très-cher Père,

I have this moment heard tidings which distress me exceedingly, and the more so that your last letter led me to suppose you were so well; but I now hear that you are really ill. I need not say how anxiously I shall long for a better report of you to comfort me, and I do hope to receive it, though I am always prone to anticipate the worst. As death (when closely considered) is the true goal of our life, I have made myself so thoroughly acquainted with this good and faithful friend of man, that not only has its image no longer anything alarming to me, but rather something most peaceful and consolatory; and I thank my heavenly Father that He has vouchsafed to grant me the happiness, and has given me the opportunity (you understand me), to learn that it is the *key* to our true felicity. I never lie down at night without thinking that (young as I am) I may be no more before the next morning dawns. And yet not one of all those who know me can say that I ever was morose or melancholy in my intercourse with them. I daily thank my Creator for such a happy frame of mind, and wish from my heart that every one of my fellow-creatures may enjoy the same. In the letter that Storace took charge of [but never could subsequently find] I explained my sentiments on this point, at the time of the death of my dearest and best friend Count von Hatzfeld. He was only one-and-thirty, just the same age as myself. I do not grieve for *him*, but deeply for myself, and all those who knew him as well as I did. I hope and trust that even while I am writing this you may be recovering; if, however, contrary to my expectation, you do not feel better, I implore you, by all you hold sacred, not to conceal it from me, but either to write me the exact truth yourself, or cause some one else to do so, that I may be in your arms with as much speed as possible. I entreat you to do this by all that is holy in our eyes. But I hope soon to have a consolatory letter from you, and in this agreeable hope my wife and Carl and I kiss your hands a thousand times, and I am ever your dutiful son.

Mozart to Baron Gottfried von Jacquin
Vienna?, end of May 1787

Dearest Friend!

Please tell Herr Exner to come at nine o'clock tomorrow morning to bleed my wife.

I send you herewith your Amynt and the sacred song. Please be so good as to give the sonata to your sister with my compliments and tell her to tackle it at once, for it is rather difficult. Adieu. Your true friend

Mozart

I inform you that on returning home today I received the sad news of my most beloved father's death. You can imagine the state I am in.

Mozart to his Sister

Vienna, 2 June 1787

Dearest Sister!

You can easily imagine, as our loss is equally great, how pained I was by the sad news of the sudden death of our dearest father. Since at the moment it is impossible for me to leave Vienna (which I would the more gladly do to have the pleasure of embracing you) and since it would be hardly worth my while to do so for the sake of our late father's estate, I must confess that I too am entirely of your opinion about having a public auction. Before it takes place I should like to see the inventory, so as to be able to choose some personal effects. But if, as Herr d'Yppold has written to tell me, there is a dispositio paterna inter liberos, then, of course, I must be informed of this dispositio beforehand, so as to be able to make further arrangements; – hence I am now expecting an accurate copy of it and after a rapid perusal of its contents I shall let you have my opinion at once – Please see that the enclosed letter is handed to our kind and sincere friend Herr d'Yppold. As he has already proved his friendship to our family on so many occasions, I trust that he will again be a friend to me also and act for me in any necessary events. Farewell, dearest sister! I am ever your faithful brother

W. A. Mozart

P.S. – My wife wishes to be remembered to you and your husband, and so do I.

Mozart to Baron Gottfried von Jacquin, Vienna
Prague, 4 November 1787

My dearest and best Friend,

I hope you received my letter. My opera, 'Don Giovanni', was given here on the 29th of October, with the most brilliant success. Yesterday it was performed for the fourth time (for my benefit). I think of leaving this on the 12th or 13th. When I return, you shall have the aria to sing. – N.B. *Entre nous*, I do wish that some of my good friends (particularly Bridi* and you) could be here even for one evening to share my pleasure. *Perhaps it may yet be given in Vienna* – I wish it may. Every effort has been made here to persuade me to remain for a couple of months, and to write another opera, but however flattering the proposal may be, I cannot accept it. Now tell me, my dear friend, how you are. I hope you

---

* A young Novoredo banker, who was very intimate with Mozart, and in March 1786 appeared in a private performance of 'Idomeneo' with Mozart. He subsequently erected, in his garden at Novoredo, a monument to Mozart with this inscription, 'Master of the soul by the power of melody.'

are all as well as we are. You cannot fail to be happy, for you possess everything that you can wish for at your age, and in your position – especially as you now seem to have entirely given up your former excited mode of life. Do you not every day become more convinced of the truth of the little lectures I used to inflict on you? Are not the pleasures of a transient capricious passion widely different from the happiness produced by rational and true love? I feel sure that you often in your heart thank me for my admonitions. I shall feel quite proud if you do. But, jesting apart, you do really owe me some little gratitude if you are become worthy of Fräulein N——, for I certainly played no insignificant part in your improvement or reform.

My great-grandfather used to say to his wife, my great-grandmother, who in turn told her daughter, my mother, who repeated it to her daughter, my own sister, that it was a very great art to talk eloquently and well, but an equally great one to know the right moment to stop. I, therefore, shall follow the advice of my sister, thanks to our mother, grandmother, and great-grandmother, and thus end not only my moral ebullition, but my letter.

9th November. – It was quite an unexpected pleasure to me to receive your letter of the 2nd. If the song in question be required to prove my friendship for you, you have no further cause to doubt it, for here it is. [Köchel, No. 530]. But I trust that, even *without the song*, you

are convinced of my true friendship, and in this hope
I remain ever your sincere friend,

W. A. Mozart

P.S. – How is it that neither your parents nor your
brother and sister have sent me any remembrances? I
cannot understand it. I attribute it, however, my dear
friend, to your own forgetfulness, and I flatter myself
that I am not mistaken as to this. The double seal was
owing to this: the red wax was good for nothing, so I
put black wax on the top of it. And as for my usual seal,
I forgot to bring it from Vienna. Adieu! I hope soon to
embrace you. Our united regards to your whole family
and to the Nattorps.

Mozart to Michael Puchberg

Vienna, before 17 June 1788

My dear esteemed Friend and O. B.,

The conviction that you are a true friend of mine, and
that you know me to be an honourable man, gives me
courage to open my whole heart to you, and to make
the following request. Without any further preamble,
and with my natural straightforwardness, I proceed at
once to state the case. If you have sufficient regard and
friendship for me to succour me by the loan of one or
two thousand gulden for a couple of years, at the usual
rate of interest, you would extricate me from a mass of
troubles. You, no doubt, yourself know how difficult –

nay, impossible – it is to pay your way when obliged to wait for the receipt of various sums, without a certain, or, at all events, the most needful, amount of cash in hand; without this there can be no regulation in one's affairs; nothing can come of nothing. If you do me this friendly service, having then some money to go on with, I can, in the first place, more easily manage the necessary outlay at the proper time, the payment of which I am now obliged to defer, and thus am often forced to pay away all I receive at the most inconvenient time; secondly, I can also work with a mind more free from care and with a lighter heart, and thus earn more. I do not believe that you can have any doubts of your safety in making this loan. You know pretty well how I stand, and also my principles. You need not be uneasy about the subscription; I am only prolonging the time for a few months, in the hope of finding more lovers of music elsewhere than here. I have now opened my whole heart to you on a matter of the greatest importance to me. I shall anxiously expect your reply, which I do hope may be favourable. I don't know, still I take you to be a man who, like myself, will, if possible, succour a friend – a true friend.

If it should so happen that you find it inconvenient to part with so large a sum at once, I beg you, at all events, to lend me a couple of hundred gulden, because my landlord in the Landstrasse was so pressing that I was obliged to pay him on the spot (in order to avoid anything unpleasant), which has caused me great embarrassment.

We sleep tonight in our new apartments for the first time, and we mean to remain there both summer and winter. I think this, after all, quite as well, if not better, for I have not much to do in the town, and shall not be exposed to so many visits, so I can work harder; and if business compels me to go into the town, which is not likely often to be the case, any fiacre will take me there for ten kreuzers. This apartment is not only cheaper, but far more agreeable in spring, summer, and autumn, especially as I have a garden. My house is in the Währinger Gasse, bei den 5 Sternen, No. 135. Pray consider my letter as a proof of my sincere reliance on you, and believe me, till death, your true and attached friend,

W. A. Mozart

P.S. – When are you likely to have a little music again in your house? I have written a new trio [in E major: Köchel, No. 542].

[Puchberg has marked on this letter, '17th June, 1788, sent 200 florins.']

Mozart to Michael Puchberg
Vienna, beginning of July 1788

Dearest Friend and B.O.,

Owing to great difficulties and complications my affairs have become so involved that it is of the utmost importance to raise some money on these two pawn-broker's tickets. In the name of our friendship I implore you to do me this favour; but you must do it immediately. Forgive my importunity, but you know my situation. Ah! If only you had done what I asked you! Do it even now – then everything will be as I desire.

Ever your Mozart

Mozart to Franz Hofdemel
Vienna, end of March 1789

Dearest Friend!

I am taking the liberty of asking you without any hesitation for a favour. I should be very much obliged to you if you could and would lend me a hundred gulden until the 20th of next month. On that day I receive the quarterly instalment of my salary and shall then repay the loan with thanks. I have relied too much on a sum of a hundred ducats due to me from abroad. Up to the present I have not yet received it, although I am expecting it daily. Meanwhile I have left myself too short of cash, so that I urgently need some ready money and have therefore appealed to your goodness, for I am absolutely convinced of your friendship.

Well, we shall soon be able to call one another by a *more delightful name!* For your novitiate is very nearly at an end!

Mozart

Mozart to his Wife

We expected to be in Dresden on Saturday after dinner, but did not arrive till yesterday – the roads were so bad. I went to Neumann's yesterday [one of the secretaries at the War Office], where Madame Duschek lives, to give her Duschek's letter. Her lodging is on the third floor in an alley, and from her room you can see all who are coming. When I arrived at the door, Herr Neumann was already there, and asked me whom he had the honour to address. I replied, 'I will tell you presently who I am, but first be so good as to call out Madame Duschek' (in order not to spoil my fun), but at the same moment Madame Duschek stood before me, having recognised me from her window, when she at once said, 'I see some one coming who looks very like Mozart.' All was now joy. The party was large, and consisted entirely of ladies, most of whom were very plain, but they made up for their want of beauty by their amiability. The Prince and I are going to breakfast there today; we then visit Naumann [Capellmeister], and afterwards hear the Elector's private band. We leave this for Leipzig tomorrow or next day. After getting this letter, address to me, Poste Restante, Berlin. I hope you got my letter from Prague. The Neumanns and the Duscheks send you their regards, and also to Lange and your sister.

My darling wife, would that I had a letter from you.

If I were to tell you all my follies about your dear portrait, it would make you laugh. For instance, when I take it out of its case, I say to it, God bless you, my Stanzerl! God bless you, Spitzbub, Krallerballer, Spitzignas, Bagatellerl, schluck und druck!* and when I put it away again, I let it slip gently into its hiding-place, saying, Now, now, now! but with an appropriate emphasis on this significant word; and at the last one I say quickly, Good night, darling mouse, sleep soundly! I know I have written something very foolish (for the world at all events), but not in the least foolish for us, who love each other so fondly. This is the sixth day that I have been absent from you, and, by heavens! it seems to me a year. You may often have some difficulty in reading my letters, because, writing hurriedly, I write badly. Adieu, my only love! The carriage is waiting, but on this occasion I cannot say, 'Well done! the carriage is here'; but *male*. Farewell! and love me as I shall ever love you. I send you a million of the most tender kisses, and am ever your fondly loving husband,

W. A. Mozart

P.S. – How is our Carl? well, I hope? Kiss him for me. Kind regards to the Puchbergs. – N.B. You must not take my letters as patterns for yours; the only reason mine are so short is because I am so hurried, or I would cover a whole sheet of paper, but you have more leisure. Adieu!

* These words occur in a jocose canon of Mozart's.

Mozart to his Wife
Dresden, 16 April 1789

My darling sweet little Wife,

... Darling wife, I have a number of requests to make to you:–

1st. I beg you will not be melancholy.

2nd. That you will take care of yourself, and not expose yourself to the spring breezes.

3rd. That you will not go out to walk alone – indeed, it would be better not to walk at all.

4th. That you will feel entirely assured of my love. I have not written you a single letter without placing your dear portrait before me.

5th. I beg you not only to be careful of your honour and mine in your conduct, but to be equally guarded as to *appearances*. Do not be angry at this request; indeed, it ought to make you love me still better, from seeing the regard I have for my honour.

6th. Lastly, I wish you would enter more into details in your letters. I should like to know whether my brother-in-law, Hofer, arrived the day that I set off; whether he comes often, as he promised he would; whether the Langes call on you; whether the portrait is progressing; what your mode of life is – all things which naturally interest me much. Now farewell, my best beloved! Remember that every night before going to bed I converse with your portrait for a good half-hour, and the same when I awake. We set off on the 18th, the day after tomorrow. Continue to write to me, Poste Restante, Berlin. I kiss and embrace you 1,095,060,437,082 times (this will give you a fine opportunity to exercise yourself in counting), and am ever your most faithful husband and friend,

W. A. Mozart

The account of the close of our Dresden visit shall follow next time. Good night!

Mozart to his Wife
Berlin, 19 May 1789

Dearest, most beloved little Wife of my Heart!

Well, I trust that you will by now have received some letters from me, for they can't all have been lost. This time I can't write very much to you, as I have to pay some calls and I am only sending this to announce my arrival. I shall probably be able to leave by the 25th; at least I shall do my best to do so. But I shall let you know definitely before then. I shall quite certainly get away by the 27th. Oh, how glad I shall be to be with you again, my darling! But the first thing I shall do is to take you by your front curls; for how on earth could you think, or even imagine, that I had forgotten you? How could I possibly do so? For even *supposing* such a thing, you will get on the very first night a thorough spanking on your dear little kissable arse, and this you may count upon.

Adieu.

> Ever your only friend and your husband
> who loves you with all his heart
> > *W. A. Mozart*

Mozart to Michael Puchberg
Vienna, second half of July 1789

Dearest Friend and Brother!

Since the time when you rendered me that great and friendly service, I have been living in such *misery*, that for very grief not only have I not been able to go out, but I could not even write.

At the moment she is easier, and if *she had not contracted bed-sores*, which make her condition most wretched, she would be able to sleep. The only fear is that the bone may be affected. She is extraordinarily resigned and awaits recovery or death with true philosophic calm. My tears flow as I write. Come and see us, most beloved friend, if you can; and, *if you can*, give me your advice and help *in the matter you know of*.

> *Mozart*

Mozart to his Wife at Baden
Vienna, first half of August 1789

Dearest little Wife!

I was delighted to get your dear letter – and I trust that you received yesterday my second one together with the infusion, the electuaries and the ants' eggs. I shall sail off to you at five o'clock tomorrow morning. Were it not for the joy of seeing you again and embracing you, I should not drive out to Baden just yet, for 'Figaro' is going to be performed very soon, and as I have some alterations to make, my presence will be required at the rehearsals. I shall probably have to be back here by the 19th. But to stay here until the 19th *without you* would be quite impossible. Dear little wife! I want to talk to you quite frankly. You have no reason whatever to be unhappy. You have a husband who loves you and does all he possibly can for you. As for your foot, you must just be patient and it will surely get well again. I am glad indeed when you have some fun – of course I am – but I do wish that you would not sometimes make yourself so cheap. In my opinion you are too free and easy with N.N. [name erased] … and it was the same with N.R., when he was still at Baden. Now please remember that they are not half so familiar with other women, whom they perhaps know more intimately, as they are with you. Why, N.N. who is usually a well-conducted fellow and particularly respectful to women, must have been misled by your behaviour into writing the most disgusting and most impertinent sottises which he put into his letter. A woman must always make herself respected, or else people will begin to talk about her. My love! Forgive me for being so frank, but my peace of mind demands it as well as our mutual happiness. Remember that you yourself once admitted to me that you were inclined to *give way too easily*. You know the consequences of that. Remember too the promise you gave to me. Oh, God, do try, my love! Be merry and happy and charming to me. Do not torment yourself and me with unnecessary jealousy. Believe in my love, for surely you have proofs of it, and you will see how happy we shall be. Rest assured that it is only by her prudent behaviour that a wife can enchain her husband. Adieu. Tomorrow I shall kiss you most tenderly.

Mozart

Mozart to Archduke Francis
Vienna, during the first half of May 1790

I am so bold as to entreat your Royal Highness to present to his Majesty, with your sanction, this humble petition. Desire of fame, love of work, and the conviction of my capabilities, all embolden me to presume to apply for a second situation as Capellmeister, especially as that very able Capellmeister, Salieri, has never devoted himself to church music, whereas I from my youth have carefully acquired this style. The reputation I enjoy in the world for my pianoforte-playing makes me venture to solicit also the honour of being appointed musical instructor to the Royal Family.

Persuaded that I have applied to a most kind and

gracious patron, I shall live in the hope of a favourable result, and shall assuredly strive by my industry, zeal, fidelity, and integrity, always to &c., &c.

Mozart to his Wife at Baden
Vienna?, 2 June 1790

Dearest little Wife!

I hope that you have received my letter. Well, I must scold you a little, my love! Even if it is not possible for you to get a letter from me, you could write all the same; for must all your letters be *replies* to mine? I was most certainly expecting a letter from my dear little wife – but unfortunately I was mistaken. Well, you must make it up to me and I advise you to do so, otherwise I shall never, never forgive you. Yesterday I was at the second part of 'Cosa rara', but I did not like it as much as 'Die Antons'. If you return to Vienna on Saturday, you will be able to spend Sunday morning here. We have been invited to a service and to lunch at Schwechat. Adieu – Take care of your health. *A propos.* N.N. (you know whom I mean) is a beast. He is very pleasant to my face, but he runs down 'Figaro' in public – and has treated me most abominably in the matters you know of – *I know it for certain.*

Your husband, who loves you with all his heart,

Mozart

Mozart to his Wife

Vienna, 7 June 1791

Dearest, most beloved little Wife!

I simply cannot describe my joy at receiving your last letter of the 6th, which told me that you are well and in good health, and that, very sensibly, you are not taking baths every day. Heavens! How delighted I should have been if you had come to me with the Wildburgs! Indeed I was furious with myself for not telling you to drive into town – but I was afraid of the expense. Yet it would have been *charmant* if you had done so. At five o'clock tomorrow morning, we are all driving out, three carriages of us, and so between nine and ten I expect to find in your arms all the joy which only a man can feel who loves his wife as I do! It is only a pity that I can't take with me either the clavier or the bird! That is why I would rather have gone out alone; but, as it is, I can't get out of the arrangement without offending the company.

I lunched yesterday with Süssmayr at the 'Ungarische Krone', as I still had business in town at one o'clock, – as S— has to lunch early and Mme S—, who wanted me very much to lunch with them one of these days, had an engagement at Schönbrunn. Today I am lunching with Schikaneder, for you know, you too were invited.

So far I have heard nothing from Mme Duschek; but

I shall enquire again today. I can't find out anything about your dress, as I have not seen the Wildburgs since. If it is at all possible, I shall certainly bring your hat with me. Adieu, my little sweetheart. I simply cannot tell you how I am looking forward to tomorrow. Ever your

Mozart

Mozart to his Wife
Vienna, 11 June 1791

Ma très chere Epouse!

Criés avec moi contre mon mauvais sort! Mlle Kirchgessner ne donne pas son academie lundi! Par consequent j'aurais pu vous posseder, ma chère, tout ce jour de dimanche. Mercredi je viendrai sûrement.

I must hurry, as it is already a quarter to seven – and the coach leaves at seven. When you are bathing, do take care not to slip and never stay in alone. If I were you I should occasionally omit a day in order not to do the cure too violently. I trust that someone slept with you last night. I cannot tell you what I would not give to be with you at Baden instead of being stuck here. From sheer boredom I composed today an aria for my opera [*Die Zauberflöte*]. I got up as early as half past four. Wonderful to relate, I have got back my watch – but – as I have no key, I have unfortunately not been able to wind it. What a nuisance! Schlumbla! That is a word to ponder on. Well, I wound *our big clock* instead. Adieu – my love! I am lunching today with Puchberg. I kiss you a thousand times and say with you in thought: 'Death and despair were his reward!'

Ever your loving husband

W. A. Mozart

See that Carl behaves himself. Give him kisses from me.

Take an electuary if you are constipated – not otherwise. Take care of yourself in the morning and evening, if it is chilly.

Mozart to his Wife
Vienna, 25 June 1791

Ma très chere Épouse!

I have this moment received your letter, which has given me extraordinary pleasure. I am now longing for a second one to tell me how the baths are affecting you. I too am sorry not to have been present yesterday at your fine concert, not on account of the music, but because I should have been so happy to be with you. I gave ... a surprise today. First of all I went to the Rehbergs. Well, Frau Rehberg sent one of her daughters upstairs to tell him that a dear old friend had come from Rome and had searched all the houses in the town without being able to find him. He sent down a message to say, please would I wait for a few minutes. Meanwhile the poor fellow put on his Sunday best, his finest clothes, and turned up with his hair most elaborately dressed. You can imagine how we made fun of him. I can never resist making a fool of someone – if it is not ..., then it must be ... or Snai. And where did I sleep? At home, of course. And I slept very well, except that the mice kept me most excellent company. Why, I had a first-rate argument with them. I was up before five o'clock. A propos, I advise you not to go to Mass tomorrow. Those peasants are too cheeky for my taste. True, you have a rough *compagnon*, but the peasants don't respect him, *perdunt respectum*, as they see at once that he is a silly ass – Snai!

I shall give a verbal reply to Süssmayr. I would rather not waste paper on him.

Tell Krügel or Klüsel that you would like to have better food. Perhaps, when you are passing, you could speak to him yourself. That would be even better. He is a good fellow otherwise and respects me.

Tomorrow I shall join the procession to the Josef-stadt, holding a candle in my hand! – Snai!

Do not forget my warnings about the morning and evening air and about bathing too long. My kind regards to Count and Countess Wagensperg. Adieu. I kiss you one thousand times in thought and am ever your

Mozart

P.S. – Perhaps after all it would be well to give Carl

a little rhubarb. Why did you not send me that long letter? Here is a letter for him – I should like to have an answer. Catch – Catch – bis – bis – bs – bs – kisses are flying about for you – bs – why, another one is hobbling after the rest!

I have this moment received your second letter. Beware of the baths! And do sleep more – and not so irregularly, or I shall worry – I am a little anxious as it is.

Adieu.

Mozart to Michael Puchberg
Vienna, 25 June 1791

Dearest and best Friend and Brother,

Business prevented my having the pleasure of calling on you today. I have a request to make. My wife writes to me that she can see (although he has no right yet to demand it) that her landlord would be glad to receive some money for her lodgings as well as for her board, and she begs me to send her some. Supposing that it would be time enough to provide for this at the moment of her departure, I am not a little perplexed. I do not wish to expose my wife to anything at all disagreeable, and yet I must not leave myself entirely without money. If you, my dear friend, can supply me with a small sum to send to her immediately, you will exceedingly oblige me.* I only require the loan for a

* Puchberg's note is, 'Sent twenty-five florins same day.'

few days, when you shall receive 2,000 florins in my name, from which you can at once repay yourself. Ever your

Mozart

Mozart to his Wife at Baden
Vienna, 2 July 1791

Ma très chere Epouse!

I trust that you are very well. I have just remembered that you have *very rarely* been upset during pregnancy. Perhaps the baths are too laxative? I should not wait for *certain proofs*, which would be too unpleasant. My advice is that you should stop them now! Then I should feel quite easy in my mind. Today is the day when you are not supposed to take one and yet I wager that that little wife of mine has been to the baths? *Seriously* – I had much rather you would prolong your cure well into the autumn. I hope that you got my first little note.

Please tell that fool Süssmayr to send me my score of the first act, from the introduction to the finale, so that I may orchestrate it. It would be a good thing if he could put it together today and dispatch it by the first coach tomorrow, for I should then have it at noon. I have just had a visit from a couple of Englishmen who refused to leave Vienna without making my acquaintance. But of course the real truth is that they wanted to meet that great fellow Süssmayr and only came to see me in order to find out where he lived, as they had heard that I was fortunate enough to enjoy his acquaintance. I told them to go to the 'Ungarische Krone' and to wait there until he should return from Baden! Snai! They want to engage him to clean the lamps. I am longing most ardently for news of you. It is half past twelve already and I have heard nothing. I shall wait a little longer before sealing my letter ... Nothing has come, so I must close it! Farewell, dearest, most beloved little wife! Take care of your health, for as long as you are well and are kind to me, I don't care a fig if everything else goes wrong. Follow the advice I gave you at the beginning of this letter and farewell. Adieu – a thousand kisses for you and a thousand boxes on the ear for Lacci Bacci. Ever your

Mozart

Mozart to his Wife
Vienna, 3 July 1791, Sunday

Dearest, most beloved little Wife of my heart!

I received your letter together with Montecucoli's and am delighted to hear that you are well and in good spirits. I thought as much. If you take the baths twice in succession, you will be thoroughly spanked when I come out to you again! Thanks for the finale you sent and my clothes, but I cannot understand why you did not put in a letter. I searched all the pockets in the coat and trousers. Well, perhaps the post-woman is still carrying it about in her pocket! I am only delighted that you are in good health, my dear little wife. I am sure you will follow my advice. If you do, I can feel a little calmer! As for my health, I am pretty well. I trust that my affairs will improve as rapidly as possible. Until they are settled I cannot be quite easy in my mind. But I hope to be so soon.

I trust that Süssmayr will not forget to copy out at once what I left for him; and I expect to receive today those portions of my score for which I asked. I see from . . .'s Latin letter that neither of you is drinking any wine. I don't like that. Have a word with your supervisor, who no doubt will only be too delighted to give you some on my account. It is a wholesome wine and not expensive, whereas the water is horrid. I lunched yesterday at Schikaneder's with the Lieutenant-Colonel, who is also taking the Antony baths. Today I am lunching with Puchberg. Adieu, little sweetheart. Dear Stanzi Marini, I must close in haste, for I have just heard one o'clock strike; and you know that Puchberg likes to lunch early. Adieu. Ever your

Mozart

Lots of kisses for Carl – and whippings for . . .*

---

* Probably Süssmayr.

Mozart to his Wife

Dearest, most beloved little Wife!

I have this moment returned from the opera, which was as full as ever. As usual the duet 'Mann und Weib' and Papageno's glockenspiel in Act I had to be repeated and also the trio of the boys in Act II. But what always gives me most pleasure is the *silent approval*! You can see how this opera is becoming more and more esteemed. Now for an account of my own doings. Immediately after your departure I played two games of billiards with Herr von Mozart, the fellow who wrote the opera which is running at Schikaneder's theatre; then I sold my nag for fourteen ducats; then I told Joseph to get Primus to fetch me some black coffee, with which I smoked a splendid pipe of tobacco; and then I orchestrated almost the whole of Stadler's rondo [from K622]. Meanwhile I have had a letter which Stadler has sent me from Prague. All the Duscheks are well. I really think that she cannot have received a single one of your letters – and yet I can hardly believe it. Well, they have all heard already about the splendid reception of my German opera. And the strangest thing of all is that on the very evening when my new opera was performed for the first time with such success, 'Tito' was given in Prague for the last time with terrific applause. Bedini sang better than ever. The little duet in A major which the two maidens sing was repeated; and had not the audience wished to spare Madame Marchetti, a repetition of the rondo would have been very welcome. Cries of 'Bravo' were shouted at Stodla from the parterre and even from the orchestra – 'What a miracle for Bohemia!' he writes, 'but indeed I *did my very best.*' Stodla writes too that Süssmayr ... but I now see that he is an idiot – ..., I mean, not Stodla, who is only a bit of an idiot – but ..., why, he is a full-blown idiot. At half past five I left my room and took my favourite walk by the Glacis to the theatre. But what do I see? What do I smell? Why, here is Don Primus with the cutlets! Che gusto! Now I am eating to your health! It is just striking eleven. Perhaps you are already asleep? St! St! St! I won't wake you.

Saturday, the 8th. You should have seen me at supper yesterday! I couldn't find the old tablecloth, so I pulled out one as white as a snowdrop, and put in front of me the double candlestick with wax candles. According to Stadler's letter the Italians are done for in Vienna. Further, Madame Duschek must have got *one* letter from you, for he says: 'The lady was very well pleased with Mathies' postscript. She said: "I like the ASS, or A-S-S, as he is".' Do encourage ... to write something for ..., for he has begged me very earnestly to see to this. As I write, no doubt you will be having a good swim. The friseur came punctually at six o'clock. At half past five Primus had lit the fire and he then woke me up at a quarter to six. Why must it rain just now? I did so much hope that you would have lovely weather. Do keep very warm, so that you may not catch a cold. I hope that these baths will help you to keep well during the winter. For only the desire to see you in good health made me urge you to go to Baden. I already feel lonely without you. I knew I should. If I had had nothing to do, I should have left at once to spend the week with you, but I have *no facilities for working at Baden*, and I am anxious, as far as possible, to avoid all risk of *money difficulties*. For the most pleasant thing of all is to have a mind at peace. To achieve this, however, one must work hard; and I like hard work. Give ... a few sound boxes on the ear from me, and I ask ..., whom I kiss a thousand times, to give him a couple too. For Heaven's sake do not let him starve in this respect. The last thing in the world I could wish would be his reproach that you had not treated or looked after him properly. Rather give him too many blows than too few. It would be a good thing if you were to leave a bump on his nose, or knock out an eye, or inflict some other visible injury, so that the fellow may never be able to deny that he has got something from you.

Adieu, dear little wife! The coach is just going. I trust that I shall have a letter from you today and in this sweet hope I kiss you a thousand times and am ever

your loving husband

W. A. Mozart

Mozart to his Wife

Vienna, 8–9 October 1791, Saturday night at half past ten o'clock

My darling sweet Wife,

On my return from the opera, to my great joy and delight, I found your letter. Although Saturday, being post-day, is never a good opera night, still mine was crowded this evening, and performed with the usual applause and encores. It is to be repeated tomorrow, but suspended on Monday; so Stoll must manage to come on Tuesday, when it will be given for the *first time* again; I say for the *first time*, because it will probably be performed again a number of times in succession. I have just eaten a capital slice of hare, which *Dr.* Primus (my faithful valet) found for me; and as my appetite is very good today, I sent him off again to try to get me something more, if possible, and I am writing to you meanwhile. Early this morning I set to work so busily [at the Requiem] that I did not stop till half-past one o'clock, so I went off in a great hurry to Hofer's (not wishing to dine quite alone), where I met your mamma. Immediately after dinner I went home, and wrote again till it was time to go to the opera. Leitgeb asked me to take him, which I did. Tomorrow your mamma is to go with me; Hofer has given her the libretto to read previously. We may well say of mamma that she *sees* the opera, but not that she *hears* it!

The N.N.'s had a box this evening, and heartily

applauded everything; but he, the stupid idiot, showed himself such a thorough Bavarian, that I could not stay with him, or I must have called him an ass to his face. Unluckily I was in their box when the second act began, with a very solemn scene. He laughed all through it. At first I had the patience to attract his attention to various passages, but he persisted in laughing. This was rather too much, so I called him Papageno, and took myself off; but I don't believe the thick-headed oaf understood the allusion. I went into another box where Hamm and his wife were. I had the greatest pleasure in being with them, and stayed there till the end. I went behind the scenes when Papageno's air accompanied by bells began, feeling such a strong impulse to play the bells myself for once. I played them a capital trick, for at Schikaneder's pause I made an arpeggio; he started, looked behind the scenes, and saw me. The second time the pause came, I did nothing, when he paused, and would not proceed. I guessed his thoughts, and played a chord. He then struck the bells and said *Halt's Maul!* (hold your tongue!) which made everybody laugh. I believe it was owing to this joke that many realised for the first time that Schikaneder did not himself play the instrument. You cannot think what a charming effect the music has from a box close to the orchestra, far better than from the gallery; as soon as you return you must try this.

Sunday, 7 o'clock A.M. – I have slept as soundly as possible, and hope that you have done the same.

I thoroughly enjoyed the half capon that friend Primus brought me. At ten o'clock I am going to hear mass at the monastery of the Piarists, because Leitgeb told me that I could then speak to the director [about Carl], and I shall also stay to dinner there. Primus told me yesterday that a great many people were ill in Baden. Is this true? Be very careful not to expose yourself to this stormy weather. Now comes Primus with the annoying news that the post-carriage drove off at seven o'clock this morning, and no other goes till the afternoon; so my writing late at night, and early in the morning, has been of no use. You cannot get this letter till tonight, which vexes me very much. I shall certainly come to see you next Sunday, when we can all go together to the Casino, and home on Monday. Lechleitner was again at the opera; though no great connoisseur, he is at all events a real lover of music, and this N.N. is not. He is a mere *nonentity*, and much prefers a dinner. Farewell, my darling! I send you a million of kisses. Ever your

Mozart

P.S. – Kiss Sophie from me. To Siesmag* I send two good fillips on the nose, and a hearty pull at his hair. A thousand compliments to Stoll. Adieu! 'The hour strikes! Farewell! We shall meet again!'

---

* He refers to his youngest child Wolfgang, of whom he used to prophesy that he would be a genuine Mozart, because when he cried, he always did so in the precise key in which his father chanced to be playing at the moment.

Mozart to his Wife

Vienna, 14 October 1791

Dearest, most beloved little Wife,

Hofer drove out with me yesterday, Thursday the
13th, to see our Carl.* We dined there and then we
all drove back to Vienna. At six o'clock I called in the
carriage for Salieri and Madame Cavalieri – and drove
them to my box. Then I drove back quickly to fetch
Mamma and Carl, whom I had left at Hofer's. You can't
conceive how charming they were and how much they
liked not only my music, but the libretto and everything.
They both said that it was an *operone*, worthy to be
performed for the greatest festival and before the greatest monarchs, and that they would often go to see it, as
they had never seen a more beautiful or delightful show.
Salieri listened and watched most attentively and from
the overture to the last chorus there was not a single
number that did not call forth from him a *bravo!* or *bello!*
It seemed as if they could not thank me enough for my
kindness. They had intended in any case to go to the
opera yesterday. But they would have had to be in their
places by four o'clock. As it was, they saw and heard
everything in comfort in my box. When it was over
I sent them home and then had supper at Hofer's with
Carl. Then I drove him home and we both slept soundly.

* Mozart's eldest son was at school in Perchtoldsdorf.

Carl was absolutely delighted at being taken to the opera. He is looking so well. He could not be in a better place for his health, but everything else there is wretched, alas! All they can do is to turn out a good peasant into the world. But enough of this. As his serious studies (God help them!) do not begin until Monday, I have arranged to keep him until after lunch on Sunday. I told them that you would like to see him. So tomorrow, Saturday, I shall drive out with Carl to see you. You can then keep him, or I shall take him back to Heeger's after dinner. Reflect on it. A month can hardly do him much harm. In the meantime the arrangement with the Piarists, which is now under discussion, may come to something. On the whole, Carl is no worse; but at the same time he is not one whit better than he was. He still has his old bad manners; he never stops chattering just as he used to do in the past; and he is, if anything, *less inclined to learn than before*, for out there [at Perchtoldsdorf] all he does is to run around in the garden for five hours in the morning and five hours in the afternoon, as he has himself confessed. In short, the children do nothing but eat, drink, sleep and go for walks. Leutgeb and Hofer are with me at the moment. The former is staying to supper with me. I have sent out my faithful comrade Primus to order dinner from the Bürgerspital. I am quite satisfied with the fellow. He has only let me down once, when I was obliged to sleep at Hofer's, which annoyed me intensely, as they sleep far too long there. I am happiest at home, for I am accustomed to my own hours. This one occasion put me in a very bad humour. Yesterday the whole day was taken up with that trip to Bernstorf, so I could not write to you. But your not having written to me for two days, is really unforgivable. I hope that I shall certainly have a letter from you today, and that tomorrow I shall talk to you and embrace you with all my heart.

Farewell. Ever your

Mozart

I kiss Sophie a thousand times. Do what you chose with N.N. Adieu.

Mozart died on 5 December 1791. Among those who attended him in his last illness was Constanze's youngest sister, Sophie Haibel, who many years later wrote the following account in a letter to Constanze's second husband, Georg Nissen, then collecting material for his biography of Mozart.

Diakovar, 7 April 1825

Now I must tell you about Mozart's last days. Well, Mozart became fonder and fonder of our dear departed mother and she of him. Indeed he often came running along in great haste to the Wieden (where she and

I were lodging at the Goldner Pflug), carrying under his arm a little bag containing coffee and sugar, which he would hand to our dear mother, saying, 'Here, mother dear, now you can have a little "Jause".' She used to be as pleased as a child. He did this very often. In short, Mozart in the end never came to see us without bringing something.

Now when Mozart fell ill, we both made him a night-jacket which he could put on at the front, since on account of his swelling he was unable to turn in bed. Then, as we didn't know how seriously ill he was, we also made him a quilted dressing-gown (though indeed his dear wife, my sister, had given us the materials for both garments), so that when he got up he should have everything he needed. We visited him often and he was really delighted with the dressing-gown. I used to go into town every day to see him. Well, one Saturday when I was with him, Mozart said to me: 'Dear Sophie, do tell Mamma that I am fairly well and that I shall be able to go and congratulate her in the octave of her name-day.' Who could have been more delighted than I to bring such cheerful news to my mother, when she could hardly expect the news? I hurried home therefore to comfort her, the more so as he himself really seemed to be bright and happy. The following day was a Sunday. I was young then and rather vain, I admit, and liked to dress up. But I never cared to go out walking from our suburb into town in my fine clothes, and I had no money for a drive. So I said to our good mother: 'Dear Mamma, I'm not going to see Mozart today. He was so well yesterday that surely he will be even better today, and one day more or less won't make much difference.' Well, my mother said: 'Listen to me. Make me a cup of coffee and then I'll tell you what you ought to do.' She was rather inclined to keep me at home; and indeed my sister knows how much I had to be with her. I went into the kitchen. The fire was out. I had to light the lamp and make a fire. All the time I was thinking of Mozart. I had made the coffee and the lamp was still burning. Then I noticed how wasteful I had been with my lamp, I mean, that I had burned so much wax. It was still burning brightly. I stared into the flame and thought to myself, 'How I should love to know how Mozart is.' While I was thinking and gazing at the flame, it went out, as completely as if the lamp had never been burning. Not a spark remained on the big wick and yet there wasn't the slightest draught – that I can swear to. A terrible feeling came over me. I ran to our mother and told her all. She said, 'Well, take off your fine clothes and go into town and bring me back news of him at once. But be sure not to tarry.' I hurried along as fast as I could. Alas, how frightened I was when my sister, who was almost despairing and yet trying to keep calm, came out to me, saying: 'Thank God that you have come, dear Sophie. Last night he was so ill that I thought he would not be alive this morning. Do stay with me today, for if he has another bad turn, he will pass away tonight. Go in to him for a little while and see how he is.' I tried to control myself and went to his bedside. He immediately called me to him and said: 'Ah, dear Sophie, how glad I am that you have come. You must stay here tonight and see me die.' I tried hard to be brave and to persuade him that he would not. But to all my attempts he only replied: 'Why, I have already the taste of death on my tongue.' And, 'if you do not stay, who will support my dearest Constanze if you don't stay here?' 'Yes, yes, dear Mozart,' I assured him, 'but I must first go back to our mother and tell her that you would like me to stay with you today. Otherwise she will think that some disaster has befallen you.' 'Yes, do so,' said Mozart, 'but be sure and come back soon.' Good God, how distressed I felt! My poor sister followed me to the door and begged me for Heaven's sake to go to the priests at St. Peter's and implore one of them to come to Mozart – a chance call, as it were. I did so, but for a long time they refused to come and I found it difficult to persuade one of those clerical brutes to go to him. Then I ran off to my mother who was anxiously awaiting me. It was already dark. Poor woman, how shocked she was! I persuaded her to go and spend the night with her eldest daughter, the late Josepha Hofer. I then ran back as fast as I could to my distracted sister. Süssmayr was at Mozart's bedside. The well-known Requiem lay on the quilt and Mozart was explaining to him how, in his opinion, he ought to finish it, when he was gone. And then he urged his wife to keep his death a secret until she should have informed Albrechtsberger, for the post should be his before God and the world. A long search was made for Dr. Closset, who was found at the theatre, but who had to wait for the end of the play. He came and ordered *cold* poultices to be placed on Mozart's burning head, which, however, affected him to such an extent that he became unconscious and remained so until he died. His last movement was an attempt to say something about the drum passages in the Requiem. That I can still hear. Müller from the Art Gallery came and took a cast of his pale, dead face. Words fail me, dearest brother, to describe how his devoted wife in her utter misery threw herself on her knees and implored the Almighty for His aid. She simply could not tear herself away from Mozart, however much I begged her to do so. If it was possible to increase her sorrow, this was done on the day after that dreadful night, when crowds of people passed by and wept and wailed for him. All my life I have never seen Mozart in a temper, still less, angry.